French Novelists

Speak Out

French Novelists

Speak Out

by

Bettina Knapp

Whitston Publishing Company
Incorporated
Troy, New York
1976

Library of Congress Catalog Card Number 75-38212

ISBN 0-87875-084-3

Printed in the United States of America

CONTENTS

PREFACE

All writing is filth
(Antonin Artaud)

It is a well-known fact that the New Novel and the New Criticism have hit it off together like soul-mates. Each has helped the other achieve recognition in its field. But this symbiotic relationship, already fading into the past, is important insofar as it hearlds "the book to come." What has happened since is this (and the implications are far-reaching): criticism, on the one hand, and creativity, on the other (if one may so designate the two poles of literary activity), have evinced a tendency to *merge their expression*. Through an overlapping of genres and roles, literature as a whole seems to be heading toward a single type of discourse. We find ourselves in the midst of a full-scale, formal upheaval. This is an ambiguous and disconcerting situation, which we should try to understand, not to condemn — especially since this crisis ("the novel is dying"/"the novel is dead") is quite possibly — at the cost of a textual revolution — the only salvation for the creative imagination.

The corpus of texts that follows offers a number of clues to the current state of French fiction. It is more pertinent to speak of "fiction" than of the "novel," for the focus of discussion is the transformation of narrative, which certain *novelists* (the term itself has acquired a multi-layered significance) are seeking to change radically, decisively, and irreversibly. The disparity among our representative group of writers serves to underscore this tendency. If the members of the "collective" *Change* (representing the *avant-garde* — in defiance of Sollers and

and company!) form a sub-group that shares similar goals, other writers, scarcely older than they, are careful to set themselves apart, if only *sotto voce*, for political as well as esthetic motives. The thesis-novel of the existentialist era has been left behind, but already there are those who decry a kind of "terrorism" among contemporary theoreticians; Robbe-Grillet, Ricardou, etc., are pilloried, like Sartre before them, but for different reasons. And the established authors, who close the roster, hardly seem to be outstripped (indeed, they often lead the way, with their perpetual search for innovation). However preoccupied all these novelists may be with language itself — linguistics having replaced psychologizing in their tool-kit — one realizes in listening to them or their juniors that what still matters most is telling, or writing "stories." The division among them is not so much in the search for modal and/or verbal originality, which sometimes degenerates into structural subtleties or plays on words (every narrative or textual system is based initially on a *gimmick*); rather, it lies in the function they ascribe to these stories vis-à-vis History.

We must not think that this scholasticism necessarily results in a new "art for art's sake." What appeals to the most imaginative and ingenious writers is the prospect of producing, through the white-heat of their writing, the image of a fascinating and complex world in travail. Hence the systematic refusal to cater to the (mental) indolence of the reader, who is required instead to lend his collaboration, as the writer tries to make him feel the *desire* that underlies their mutual endeavor. It remains to be seen whether this kind of writing can really provide "le plaisir du texte" or if the super-erudite reading that it implies is not primarily a castrating mechanism... Bettina Knapp's corpus of interviews supplies no answer. But, without being fictional or fabulous, like its "pre-text,"

I think it will furnish you considerable surprise, excite
your curiosity, and bring you satisfaction.

Marc Hanrez

(Translated by Gretchen R. Besser)

MICHEL BUTOR

INTERVIEWER'S NOTE:

Butor was born in the northern part of France, at Mons, in 1926. He studied painting, engraving, and the violin at a very early age. He took his *licence es lettres* at the Sorbonne and studied with Gaston Bachelard and Jean Wahl. In 1950 he taught in Egypt, Manchester, Salonika and Geneva. His first novel, *Milan Passage* (1954), unveiled in the minutest detail the goings on taking place in a Parisian apartment house from six o'clock until the end of the night. In *Passing Time (L'Emploi du temps)* (1965) he traced and analyzed human relationships in terms of time. Novels, essays, and analyses followed in swift succession: *A Change of Heart (La Modification)* (1957), *Degrees* (1960), *The Genius of the Place (Le Génie du lieu)* (1958, rev. 1971), *Extraordinary Study* (1961), *Words and Painting* (1969), etc.

Butor does not consider the novel to be a simple pastime. It should be looked upon as a type of "puzzle," a "mythology difficult to unravel." Neither plot nor character analyses are important as far as he is concerned. Butor's goal is to discover the secret, the nearly mathematical order, which lies hidden behind the world of reality.

Q. Has your work evolved in terms of your aesthetic, philosophical, and psychological conceptions?

A.   I began, as you know, by writing numerous poems. Some appeared in the collection, *The Outskirts from Dawn to Daybreak (La Banlieue de l'Aube a l'Aurore)*, and in the first part of *Approach Works (Travaux d'Approche)*. I also wrote, at the same time, some essays which I revised for the most part in *Repertoire I*. I was studying philosophy at the time. The novel was a means of assembling all of this knowledge and material. Yet, there was a period during which I thought I couldn't write one line of a novel, each word being the problematical outcome of the other. But, after a certain time, I was asked to look over my old poems. I copied some of them and wrote others which were entirely different. In this endeavor, I collaborated with painters and photographers. *Illustrations I* was the outcome. At the same time, I found myself writing more and more essays. The novel really represented only one portion of my literary activity. Thereafter, my work developed like a tree with many branches, each corresponding to a different *genre*. Other branches began growing in the space left vacant by the first. It has become more and more difficult to classify my writings in terms of the old categories.

Q.   Travel has played a great role in your philosophy of life and of literature. *The Genius of the Place* assembles different texts: portraits of Egypt, Cordova, Istanbul, Salonika, Delphos, Ferrara, Mantau. What is your view of travel in terms of the writer?

A.   I spoke at length on this subject in my essay, *Voyage and Writing (Le Voyage et l'Ecriture)*, which was published in *Romantisme* and in *Repertorie IV*.

Q.   Claude Mauriac wrote about your passion for traveling: "He tries to adapt his technique to the novelty and the complexity of what he has learned and understood." Can you explain Mauriac's point of view?

Does travel answer a deep need within you?

A.   Travel does fill an inner necessity within me. I must think about the other side of a decor or of a horizon to know all about the place in which I am located, but in terms of another land – of elsewhere. Every trip that I have ever taken has taught me something and has forced me to alter my writing. But one must also permit travel to take its time, to flower after one's return. The knowledge and experiences gleaned during one's voyages must ripen and mature. In some cases I had to let the fruits of certain explorations grow to maturity without ever using them. I am leaving in a month for a long voyage throughout America. I am certain that this trip will open new vistas and will enlarge my conceptions concerning your continent and my own. I hope that upon my return to Nice I shall have the tranquillity necessary to reap the benefits of this trip and have the necessary time to permit everything I have learned to flourish and to burgeon.

Q.   The second volume of *The Genius of the Place*, entitled *Where*, includes a long poem concerning France, New Mexico, and particularly the Zuni Indians. What do you find particularly interesting in the Zuni culture and rituals? Is there a link between their primitive rituals and those of the Christian religion?

A.   All civilizations fascinate me. The so-called primitive civilizations, that is to say, these societies which are made up of few people, are more readily understandable. The Zuni civilization is remarkably spectacular and I had the opportunity of observing some of their ceremonies. I try to take an ethnographic point of view of my own civilization (loosely speaking, the Christian) in order to understand it by way of comparison.

Q.   Xavier Delcourt wrote in *La Quinzaine littéraire*, about your *Approach Works*, that your "books resist all reading habits (even the new ones) and demand the reader's participation which those who have made a routine of reading are not yet ready to accept." Do you agree with him? Why?

A.   Xavier Delcourt's judgment is very flattering as far as my writing is concerned. My novels and essays use the readers' habits in order to change them. It is certainly a normal reaction on the part of readers to resist change. The reader realizes that he is altering his civilization — and totally so — by changing his reading habits. Such are the stakes.

Q.   In *Approach Works* you included three series of texts which represented three periods in the earth's evolution: The Eocene, the Miocene, and the Pliocene. Can you tell us something about this work?

A.   The three periods mentioned precede man's apparition on earth. Etymologically speaking, Eocene, Miocene and Pliocene may be defined as ancient, middle and modern periods. There is also a play on these words in French in terms of our economic and educational systems: the third or tertiary period may be placed in opposition to primary and secondary education, etc. My poetry, then, is really an attempt on my part to prepare for the coming of *real* man, of a history which would be less unfortunate than the one we know. If such were possible, then our world would merely be looked upon as a far away period, some place in pre-history.

       In the Eocene section of the volume, I included the poems I wrote during my student years, before I attempted any novels. I changed very little in terms of the poems themselves – only the way they were placed on the page. In the original texts, which some of my friends now have, and these were written some time back, I had set the texts rather audaciously on the page.

In the Miocene section, I included two texts which were also published in *Illustrations II*, but in a different way. One was written for the painter, Herold, and the other for the musician, Henri Pousseur.

In the Pliocene section, new cultural elements (lists) and autobiographical information were included. The magazine, *Arc*, carried the original test.

Q.   What are your plans for the future? Will you write for the theatre?

A.   Two new volumes have been published: *Illustrations III* and *Interval*. The latter was originally a scenario, and has just been produced on French television under the title, *Enchantment*. *Repertorie IV* is finished. I have a thousand plans.

ROBERT PINGET

INTERVIEWER'S NOTE:

Robert Pinget was born in Geneva in 1920. After receiving his law degree, he moved to Paris where he studied painting and became a skilfull artist (1946-1950). It was only after having traveled throughout Europe, having worked in Israel on a kibbutz, and having taught drawing and French in England, that he found his real bent in the literary field. The author of several plays — *Dead Letter* (1959), *The Old Tune* (1960), *Architruc* (1961) — Pinget considers the novel, with all of its problems, to be of supreme interest to him. His novel, *The Investigation* (1962), received extremely favorable reviews from the critics; and three years later he won the Prix Femina for *Someone*. Other novels followed in swift succession: *Le Libera* (1968), *Passacaille* (1969), etc.

Pinget sums up his literary preoccupations as follows: "One thing alone interests me: to capture *the tone of a voice*. This tone is, in actuality, one of the components of my own voice which I try to isolate, then to objectify."

Q. How would you assess the *nouveau roman*? Do you belong to this school which Simone de Beauvoir refers to as *l'Ecole du regard*?

A. I certainly do not belong to "L'Ecole du regard."

If anything, I would label my writing as belonging
to "L'Ecole de l'oreille." As for the *nouveau
roman*, you recall that is a term that refers to those
writers who publish their works at the Editions de
Minuit. Each of us writes in his own personal way.
Beckett does not write as I do. My style differs
from that of Simon. Nor can you say that the *nouveau
roman* is doing this or that or is leaning in this
direction or in another. We are all going in different
directions — our own personal ones. If we have something in common, it is our need to make a "tabula
rasa" of all the psychological novels that have been
written over the past century. We each try to create
a work which is a direct expression of our time.
After all, we cannot write today as we did in Balzac's
time — not if we love literature.

Q. Do you have any special methods or techniques for
    writing your novels?

A. No. I have no techniques nor do I have any special
    method. One thing alone interests me in the novel:
    to capture *the tone of a voice*. This tone is in
    actuality one of the components of my own voice
    which I try to isolate, then to objectify. There is
    always a little bit of myself in each of my characters;
    but each element is objectified to such a degree that
    it becomes a character within itself. The servant,
    for example, in *The Investigation*, has something of
    my tone of voice in his make-up. This one part of
    myself which I isolated turned into a character.

Q. How did you remember all the details: the type of
    furniture, the arrangement of this furniture, and all
    the other objects you describe in your novel *The
    Investigation*? Did you make a sketch?

A. Yes. I made a sketch so that I could have some kind

of reference point: the street names, the paintings, the manner in which the furniture was arranged in the various homes, the houses, etc. I also made a list of all the proper names I used. After all, *The Investigation* is almost five hundred pages long. But I must say that since the novel was written rather rapidly — in the space of six months — I had the facts and details pretty well in my head. When I work, I usually work day and night with very little sleep — in one stretch.

Q. What **does** the name of your novel *Graal Flibuste* (1963) mean? Does the word "Graal" have anything to do with the Holy Grail, the cup in which Joseph caught up Christ's blood? Is the word *Graal* used with satiric intent?

A. The meaning of *Graal Flibuste* is very vague indeed. "Flibuste" is certainly a way of deriding and satirising the sacred character of the Holy Grail. But my novel was not intended as a satire of religion, *per se*, nor of the tendency people have of adoring fetishes, material objects, etc.

Q. What is the meaning of the narrator's fantastic voyage through a real and yet unreal world in *Graal Flibuste*? Who is the coachman? Are you Satirising opisodic novels?

A. The coachman's voyage has no symbolic meaning. There is — and this is a certainty — a satire of episodic novels in *Graal Flibuste*. But you must not forget that much of my work verges on the humorous. I search out plays on words, puns, the droll, *Graal Flibuste* is, in many ways, a parody of the 18th century novel: a parody from the linguistic point of view. It is the sound of the words that the characters utter which is of import to me.

In view of what I have just said, it might seem strange to you but I prefer the novel to the theatre. The theatre has always been a kind of distraction for me, a means of extricating myself or escaping from the problems of the novel, *per se*.

Q. Can you tell us in more detail exactly what you mean when you speak of searching for a "tone" which you try to objectify in your novels?

A. My unique interest in my work is the search for a *tone*. It is really a problem of form: and this, consequently, justifies my belonging to what has been called the "new novel." I would consider it completely erroneous to label me a disciple of "L'Ecole du regard." If it is a question of being objective, the ear imposes just as tyrannical requirements as the eye. Now, the tone varies from one book of mine to the next. This is the case because my search in this domain will never be ended. My lot is to choose and each time my *penchant* for the new, one tone out of thousands which my ear has recorded.

Whatever is said or *meant* does not interest me; it is *the way it is said* that does. And this *way*, once it is chosen — and this preliminary part of my work, is large and painful — will prescribe the subject and composition of my narrative. The subject, once again, leaves me indifferent. My work consists in shaping it into a certain mold; and experience has taught me that it is the form of the mold or the line which makes the cake. I am sometimes surprised when rereading what I have written, at having made this or that statement, because it just does not seem to fit into my domain. I am responsible only for the errors in tone; and there must be some, alas.

The question of the coexistence or of an understanding of form and content has recently been the object of very interesting studies. But it is of

absolutely no help to me in my work since it represents a theoretical view of the situation. It proves
to me, however, once my book is completed, that this
coexistence is the only poetic reality which exists.

Why do I speak of poetry when talking about the
novel? Because this term appears to me to suit the
work of the artisan I am. The horror I feel for the
novel, in the classical sense, compels me to use the
more general vocable, signifying poetic creation or
the contrary. I have no pretentions in this domain.

When I speak of *what my ear records* it is indeed
this spoken language or rather its non-codified syntax, espousing the least inflections of feeling, which
fascinates me. This syntax which is always evolving
and has always tried, from time immemorial, to better
adapt our language to the demands made by the
senses, is, as far as I am concerned, the only one
worthy of my interest. I am not trying to codify
it — this would be working against my interests — but
rather to speak in favor of it. And I am doing this,
nor for any intellectual reasons, but simply out of
egoism.

It seems to me in fact that artistic sensibility —
mine, consequently — is worthy of being formulated
as explicitly as possible; now, this can be accomplished only be means of words and a suitable
syntax. I say this to reassure my readers. If they
find poetical elements or psychological reality in
my books — in short, anything besides verbiage — I
won't be hurt at all.

A new point of view, a modern sensibility,
original composition can certainly be found in my
writings, but I am not responsible for all this. If I
become aware of these added elements as I advance
further along in my difficult métier, the fact still
remains that it is the *voice* of the one who is doing
the talking, and that voice alone, that captures my
interest. Our ear is a recording device as powerful

as our eye. Now, I believe I can say that our normal tone, the one, for example, we use with ourselves or with those close to us, is a sort of composite of several tones – aside from those we have inherited or find in books – recorded by us since our childhood. If it is interesting to discover this natural tone in a letter, for example, by oneself and after the fact, how much more interesting is it to analyze each of the component parts of this voice, and each in turn, to create a book. I must explain something: I have never attempted to render objectively, as on a recording machine, the sound of a stranger's voice. I have enough work in store for me trying to render my own. We find here, in particular, one of the requirements set by art, which is nothing more than to transcribe the expressions of one individual, and not to expose those of another. And it is only to the extent that the artist is ferociously himself that he expresses the society of his time. This is a banality.

I say the voice of *the one who is talking*, because my preliminary work consists in choosing the one voice which interests me at this particular time – among the component parts of my own voice – and isolating it, objectifying it until a person emerges from it, the narrator himself, with whom I become identified. That is why you will always find *je* (*I*) in all of my books; but it is a different one each time.

When I use the term, *preliminary work*, it does not really express what I mean: a kind of unconscious work which goes on during my unproductive periods or after a book has been published. These periods are more or less long and difficult to stand. The tone I choose must first ripen; at this point it is not really chosen, but rather imposes itself upon me. If I still speak of choice, it is because the different tones I have exploited up until now still sound in my ear and I am always tempted to use them over again. I do not use them from one book to another because I feel — and probably wrongly so — that I have exhausted each one of them. In any event, they bore me once I have written them down. Because of my inactivity, when I am not writing, not creating anything, the temptation still subsists, and it is difficult for me to bear. I am, therefore, dependent upon this kind of ripening during by slack periods.

It would also be incorrect to say that I find the exact tone right away. This has happened to me, but it is an exception. It is more of a tonality at the onset; or the confidence I feel in this particular tonality, which slowly takes shape, in the course of the book, as my work progresses, and which, perhaps on the last page, finally becomes a tone. In any case, the conscious realization of the accuracy of the tone — or of its approximative soundness — is reached only on the last **page**. Even if I have only had the feeling of having touched upon the right note, here and there, in the course of my work, it has encouraged me sufficiently to continue.

One thing is certain: I never know from the beginning what I am going to say. I thought this was a weakness for a long time; but there is no way I can avoid it since it also makes for my only **strength**, the one which compels me to pursue my art. The discovery of something on each line was a joy in the past. Today, it is a chore; nonetheless, it still remains a discovery.

I must add that I have become more and more obsessed with my work — that is, with matters of composition. I did not have this attitude at the beginning. I maintain that from the very outset, and for each of my books, the composition is unforseeable. I become aware of it only little by little, sometimes going so far as to help it along; and this may not be the best part of my work. My confidence in the mechanical nature of the subconscious to furnish me with the essentials for my book is unshakable.

People have spoken about a *plot* in my books. I would rather use the term *situation*, dictated to me by the tone I have chosen. If a plot seems to emerge, it is only because the thread woven into the narration cannot unwind into a void. They sustain each other mutually. This narrative then will be made up of stories. If I say that these stories do not interest me, it is because I know they could have been entirely different. This does not mean that I have not accepted them, even liked them, just as I would have liked any others that still remain to be treated.

Once the time for writing has actually arrived, I consciously release the mechanism, or, if you will, the subconscious faucet — the sensation. This work is completely voluntary. You might call it a kind of automatic writing carried out in a state of total consciousness: the immediate filtering of all the possibilities that can be developed and which I try to develop only minimally, since I feel such disgust for developments in general, and for the novel in particular. Why this ascesis? To discover, in the last analysis, a silly moral truth: my own; one which is so deeply entrenched beneath a host of contradictions that only art can show me the way.

If I have not as yet found — or if my search which includes only a few years of literary exercises hasn't led me to discover — a poetic form in the narrow sense of the word, it's because it seemed to me that the novel form (or, let us say, the narrative form with everything that it entails, desire for development, difficulties in analysis) was capable of forcing me to explain myself, and consequently, made it possible for me to communicate with the outside world. I'll give you an example. When I first decided to write *The Investigation*, I had nothing to say. I felt only one desire: the need to explain myself at length.   I sat down in front of my **work** table and wrote the following sentence which was addressed to me alone: *Yes or no, answer,* which meant, *out with it.*   And the answer to this sudden question released the *tone* and everything that followed in my work.   But I still persist in believing that this tone sought to emerge from among a thousand others, when I set to work.   I had to see it written in order to accept it.

JEAN DEMELIER

INTERVIEWER'S NOTE:

Jean Démelier was born in 1940 at Poitiers. He received his Licence in Letters at the University of Poitiers. Although encouraged to become a professor, after awhile he realized he was not suited to such a career. He then toyed with the idea of becoming a critic. Suddenly, the situation changed. He began the life of a wanderer — through Paris and London, in particular. His first novel, *Job's Dream* (1971), was published by Gallimard. *People in the Street (Gens de la Rue)* (1971) was printed shortly thereafter. A radio play, *Echo*, was performed. Short texts, some poems written in English have appeared in various magazines.

Q. Can you explain the themes, images, and symbols in *Job's Dream*?

A. It took me eight years to write this book. It deals with a series of concentric and excentric meta-morphoses. *Job's Dream* is made up of two long sections and a smaller part which seeks to destroy the entire literary work:

         A/ The professor of nothing
         B/ The perverted policeman
         C/ Job surrenders

    Part A projects itself on Part B. Part C attempts to destroy the entire fable and move toward the

chant, thus drawing the entire work closer to whatever light may be shed on the situation. The light
of purification through annihilation?

There are twenty-two "chapters" in all.

It is difficult for me to speak of the ensemble of
my work, or even of its separate parts. Speaking is
the opposite of writing and I am — without a doubt —the
opposite of what I DO. I don't make the slightest
effort to play the part of the "young man of letters."
I know nothing about these things.

There is, perhaps, an attempt — in my short
texts — of self-purification. If I do become pure one
day, I will finally be able to SPEAK and say what
MUST be said.

Q.   Do you dream?

A.   Yes. A great deal. With all my might, if one can
express oneself in this way. For years now not a
night has gone by that I have not dreamed, even after
a night of love making, even after having fallen
asleep drunk with fatigue, alcohol or sadness.

But I try, I try. to construct my "characters"
from numbers, from faces.

I "draw" ("puise") my characters from within
and, at the same time, I "exhaust" ("épuise") them.
Such is my drama. I believe in my characters. One
day they may end up by killing me. So much the
better? I would like to tip toward their side, to be
them. What folly it is to say such things.

I have no imagination whatsoever. I don't even
know the meaning of the word imagination.

People in the Street is made up of things, **people**,
situations, moments which I have observed — as well
as of completely abstract notions, always in an
attempt to rediscover life from the "inside."

Job's Dream is a round of cross-currents, on a
variety of levels, with variety in the punctuation

(cf. the corpuscular theory of light with its sinister and joyful play of "corpuscles" always emerging on a "wave.)" The entire work was born from something — I don't know what — something within me, alive — between my hand and my pen, and dying beneath the gaze of the eventual reader.

Q. Do your characters emerge full blown from your unconscious? from your dream world?

A. Yes. But there is also the waking dream which must be considered. Don't people dream standing upright? in the blazing sunlight?

I would like *Job's Dream* to be analyzed from a psycho-analytic point of view. I did not try to say "everything" in this little volume. Nevertheless, I tried to say everything which could not be left UNSAID. But isn't this precisely the function of the dream? to say what one cannot leave UNSAID?

Q. Are you a member of the group known as the "New Novelists?"

A. The group is already old. It was stillborn. As far as I am concerned, their writings are merely a way of commercializing or industrializing literature. This type of group crops up in all periods. Does one have to create a "theory" concerning one's writing style before one becomes senile or in the throes of one's last gasp? I don't believe so. There are "novelists" and that's all.

I am certainly not a member of this "New Novelist" group. Perhaps of "Future Novelists?" How do I know? Each writer must find his own way. He must come to grips with himself. I am trying to understand my own inclinations, my own tendencies . . . the path I must follow.

Q.   Which writer was most influential in your development as a writer?

A.   Samuel Beckett. He has been my friend now for ten years. He is my master. My confidant. He is like a second father to me. He has guided me in my work from the very outset. He introduced me to his friends, told me what texts to send to which magazines and publishers. He keeps an eye on whatever I write, on my search. His influence on me is fundamental. I do not separate Beckett, the man, from Beckett, the prodigious writer that he is. I try, as he has, to adapt to the "filth" of modern times by means of the faculty of humor. I have been trying to rediscover a certain brand of "French" humor which the French used to possess, but that was some time ago. Not an Irish humor since I am not Irish. I consider myself in terms of literature as an apprentice, a young "urchin." I have everything to learn. This learning process is slow and I try to experience it in a slower and slower manner as time goes by. Concentric slowness in order to reach a state of simultaneity with *one's-self*.

Q.   Why did you start writing novels?

A.   I'm still asking myself this same question. I dream of expressing myself, of "expressing myself!" (as lemon expresses itself via its juice), by means of aphorisms or poems; briefly, in the most concise manner. (Alas, I have written three thousand poems, all of them probably very bad since not one was ever published in France. Besides, I haven't shown them to anyone. Perhaps this is for the best.)
     The novel is obviously the opposite of an aphorism. And yet... Perhaps it takes many words to say what one cannot yet express succinctly. If only one could say Everything in Silence, alone, it

would probably be very helpful. But the novel is like a journey. One goes away. One goes as far away as possible, to the extreme limit if one can. If there is a reason for going to the extreme... I really don't know how one thing leads to another. One goes on and on probably because one feels powerless.

When I happen to glance at *Job's Dream* at times, I cannot believe I wrote the volume. I am perhaps fortunate to **have** come this far. One must be mad to write four hundred pages – the last phrase ending with "Acta est fabula." A bit mad, certainly. Yet!

I don't really believe an author "makes his way toward novel writing," but rather, the novel "imposes itself" upon the author – in the best or worst of cases.

Q. What are you working on now?

A. A short novel which I began three years ago.

Q. Do you find that your work has evolved? and its direction has changed?

A. Perhaps, in terms of "form" and the desire to destroy form is more evident in my new work than it was in *Job's Dream*. If one can speak of evolution as far as my novels are concerned, it consists in trying to discover a greater "reality," a profounder "necessity." A little play is inevitable. As for the rest, the creative process takes place in the greatest despair, I must confess. I would like to have the audacity to say that I too wish to change the world a little bit; when I say a little, it's because I know one cannot change it entirely, Just a little, no matter how small this "little" bit may be in terms of an individual's endeavor...

I have always tried, insofar as my radio plays are concerned (*Echo, Pulsion* and two more awaiting production, *Whirlwind (Coup-de-Vent)*, and *Hemomixia* (which is having problems with the censors), to create something spe-ci-fi-ca-lly for radio — a "genre." Neither theatre nor poetic recitations. My first experiences in this domain were fascinating: two or three character plays which featured such actors as Alain Cuny, Ariane Borg, Jean-Pierre Jorris, Sylvie Artel, etc.

Q. How could you define your reality?

A. I am still too young to answer this question. Perhaps I'll never be able to answer it. I believe in THE reality. That's what I would like to express some day in my works — then fiction would become Revelation.

Q. How do you feel about the Structuralists? the collective, *Change*, the magazine, *Tel Quel*?

A. To sum this trio up in a few words: Zero amount of aluminium stained with uranium. To try to be either on the outside or on the inside — one finds oneself in no place at all. TO BE ALIVE. TO BE.

Q. What are your **plans**?

A. To write a play. Until now, I have written only a one-hour play, *On the Beach*. It was performed in 1968 at the Avignon Theatre Festival. I also intend to write a volume of aphorisms, if I can. If I have the opportunity. If I cannot prevent myself from doing it. Then, perhaps another novel. How can I know where all this will lead? particularly if one does not have the "morphology" or the mentality of an *arriviste* or of a business man of "Literature?"

I don't know where I came from nor where I am going. I really would like to know the meaning of "being there," of waiting... Such is my situation now. A strange purgatory. But I'm just a little bit "me?" and what is the meaning of this giant farce? I'm still asking this question; with my feet in the mud and my head in the stars.

Q. You're also a painter?

A. Yes. I also draw. Art permits me to survive economically, to live in a less pitiful manner. The Maison de Culture of Orléans has asked me to exhibit seventy to eighty works in October 1973 — for a "Samuel Beckett Cycle." This project has made me very happy indeed. It has moved me very deeply.

JEAN CAYROL

INTERVIEWER'S NOTE:

Born in Bordeaux in 1911, Jean Cayrol expressed his love for both nature and poetry at an early age. He founded his first literary magazine, *Abeilles et Pensées*, in 1927; his second, *Les Cahiers du Fleuve*, in 1934, to which Max Jacob, Daniel Rops and Joseph Delteil contributed. *The Poems of Pastor Grimm* (1936) and *Celestial Phenomena* (1939) are but a few of the pre-World War II volumes he published. Cayrol was inducted into the French Navy, secret service division, in 1939. In 1941, he volunteered for espionage work under Colonel Rémy; on June 10, 1941, he was denounced and arrested by the Gestapo, imprisoned at Fresnes, deported to Gusen-Mathausen in 1943 and liberated in 1945.

"I belong to silence, to the shadow of my voice," wrote Cayrol in *Mirror of Redemption (Miroir de la Rédemption)* **(1944),** a phrase which could be used to describe both his concentration camp experience and the themes of his future novels. The protagonist of his trilogy, *I Shall Live the Love of Others (Je Vivrai l'Amour des autres)* (1947), wanders in and out of the pages like a shadow, a faceless, identityless **being** who attaches himself to others, lives out their lives and loves. It is in this trilogy that Cayrol draws attention to objects which emerge as living entities, injecting their personalities and their dynamism into the flow of events. *The Wind of Memory (Le Vent de la Mémoire)* (1952), *Foreign Bodies*

(Les Corps étrangers (1959), *I Still Hear Him (Je l'entends
encore)* (1968), *The Story of the Desert (Histoire du
Désert)* (1972), *The Story of the Sea (Histoire de la Mer)*
(1973) is but a slim list of the literary output in which
poetry, fantasy and deep faith co-exist. Jean Cayrol was
elected to the Goncourt Academy in 1973.

      The concentration camp experience was the most
profound in Cayrol's life. He looked upon it as a Passion
which precedes Redemption; as the agony suffered by
a Lazarus prior to his resurrection; is the torture a writer
must endure before his creation comes into being.

Q.   Maurice Nadeau wrote the following about your
       writings: "His poems and his novels were based
       upon a new vision of the world which resulted from
       his concentration camp experience and which had,
       at the same time, shattered his former feelings,
       thoughts and concepts." Do you accept this state-
       ment?

A.   Certainly, as an author once said, the concentration
       camp inmate is neither healthy nor safe. But this
       does not mean that he must survive in order to live.

       The concentration camp experience is but one
       episode in an existence and not an end in itself.

       I think it would be useful, when living an im-
       portant life, to draw the best possible consequences
       from it.

       In brief, and to give you a picture of my thoughts:
       from a Lazarus, I was able to become a Phoenix.

Q.   You received the Renaudot Prize (1947) for the first
       two volumes of your trilogy, *I Shall Live the Love
       of Others.* Can you tell us something about the
       themes of this trilogy?

A.   I took a man from zero, before his story had even
       started, and little by little I tried to give him meaning,

a name, and to make this man participate in the story. "Only the power of speech can save man: I think, therefore, I am." My hero communicates only via speech — a **repartee** with its own contradiction.

On the other hand, I try in all of my works to accomplish what could be labeled as a type of salvage work: that's why the world of objects interests me.

Q.   Love plays a primordial role in your writings. Could you talk about this aspect of your work?

A.   Nothing exists outside of Love; writing itself is an act of love and I don't see any other way of communicating with others — except by means of this exasperating or personal feeling.

At the beginning, my characters felt as though they had been contaminated by the concentration camps and approached others with difficulty. After I wrote *I Still Hear Him* (and my other books hinge on this one), the hero is finally freed from his inability to live and can once again join the community.

Q.   How do you view objects? As do the so-called New Novelists — Robbe-Grillet, Butor, Saporta, Faye?

A.   The new novelists you have just mentioned are my **friends** and for this reason I feel close to their concepts, but at the same time mine are very different. When Robbe-Grillet describes a tomato, the fruit is an autonomous entity; it will live its own existence. As far as I am concerned, the tomato begins to exist only when I grab it, when my fingers leave their impression upon it. That's how the thing becomes an object.

What I am searching for is a warm-blooded and not a cold-blooded literature.

Q.   You wrote: ''As long as the Lazarus – type character
     remains blind, that's how long the world of objects
     sees for him and retains his reflection, the lost
     meaning of the next person's world.   An object
     placed next to a being may be more revealing, more
     accesible than the person himself.'' Would you care
     to explain this idea?

A.   The Lazarus-type character is one who has been
     shocked – figuratively speaking – by some explosive
     force and who has remained dazed.

     Only when looking at an object does a relation-
     ship between the world and himself come into being.

     My character is rather clever, unsociable, dis-
     engaged.

     He is also on the watch, on the lookout but
     also misdirected. To give you an example: one day
     in the Gusen concentration camp I found a broken
     egg shell on the floor between two slabs of stone.
     At first, I did not understand how this egg shell
     could have gotten there and then, suddenly, my sensi-
     bilities were awakened: I grabbed the remains of
     the egg shell, as though it were a valuable object.
     Symbolically speaking, it represented the world for
     me; and I was moved to tears by it.

     I tried to create my universe starting from this
     egg shell.

Q.   Are you haunted by the notion of death?   How does
     this feeling manifest itself in your novels?

A.   I skirted what you call death for three years. It was
     no ordinary death, that is, the kind suffered when a
     man is gripped by illness, but on the contrary, when
     he is struck down by an unforseeable event.

     I am a primitive, like the Australian aborigine.
     I believe we communicate with what you call the
     dead by ordinary means.   I can contact ancient

Egyptians as readily as I can the actors of Japanese Noh theatre.

Life for me is a type of *transparency,* like writing; and I believe that the most important thing — and I tried to point this out — is the meaningful nature of absence and the pacific co-existence between life and death.   My deserts are peopled as are those of the Australian oborigine.

On the other hand, two years ago a writer told me something which seems essential to me: "the terrible thing is not death, but to cease living." My characters are in this situation; they are in the process of *crossing,* and this seems even more insurmountable.   Montaigne wrote: "I am not depicting the being, only his passage."   This is the real formula.

Q.   Can you discuss your concept of reality?   Does the dream play a significant role of your novels? After reading *The Story of the Desert, The Story of the Sea, The Story of the Prairies,* I wondered whether elements are as interesting to you as they were to Bachelard?

A.   I experience my reality every day: that is, as immagination.

We are living in an anti-psychological period which may mean several different things and, at the same time, may point in several directions: if you look at your newspaper, you'll find yourself in front of a kaleidoscope, ranging from the United States to China, from a crime of passion to an altruistic act, from an incomprehensible political attitude to a fascinating economic situation, etc.   Even the word now is a dream, and, I might add, baroque.

We have been living out notions which have vanished and a code of existence which is totally outmoded.   To understand modern life one must

astonish; to learn about today's world one must re-
think it. What is of interest at this time is not the
period in which we are living (already ossified), but
space. One must try to create a type of transparent
literature which will present no difficulties whatsoever in terms of its transportability in space and
its ability to pass on to others, with ease, elements
of its existence. We can no longer view the world
or the universe in its totality — only in fragments.

What interests me is what others abandon.

We no longer have any conception of beauty or of
ugliness: the commonplace has become sublime.

Everything must be *possible* in literature and
this is what I try to work for in my novels. Everything plays its part; everything creates from itself.

Q. Will you explain your new literary formula which
Etienne Balou described in *L'Express* in terms of
The Story of the Sea: "Jean Cayrol has perfected a
new literary formula which he alone knows how to
handle with such mastery: the novel, the poem and
the philosophical tale are blended into one and
along with these, the techniques of the novel, journalism, theatre, and cinematography."

A. I agree perfectly with Etienne Lalou's statement.
Today, new literary formulas can come into being.
I can make use of their secrets as well as those from
the cultures from which they emerge. The writer's
goal is to blend everything into that crucible called
imagination, or, as Camus put it, into those "burning
grasses called memory." Why not describe the world
in which we live and use the technical means at our
disposal? The novel must disengage itself from a
certain formalism and from a psychological tradition.
It must make use of mass media. All means of information must be at its disposal; distance no longer
exists; time has been turned into a kind of timetable.

My books are written so that the reader can catch his breath. I would like my books to make him feel good, to let him recapture a certain kind of mental oxygenation. To breathe in peace in a book — that's really everything.

A book must be looked upon, not in the way Marc Luhan thinks of it, as in an icon, but as a prolongation of one's own nervous system, one's aspirations as well as one's constraints: an open book — and openly. The novel today is no longer a bolted door, but within its pages live all of our knowledge as well as our hopes.

Q.   Is there a comparison to be made between Géraldine's underwater voyage as depicted in your novel, *The Story of the Sea*, and Orpheus' and Eurydice's journey?

A.   There is a relationship between Géraldine's travels and that of Orpheus and Eurydice. But in my work, there is no sense of fatality, no provocation of destiny. Each one is master of himself: you can turn around and no one will die.

Q.   What are your latest works about? How do you feel about them?

A.   I try to show how I act and how I feel vis-a-vis a book — and in what manner a book either rids itself of me or engulfs me.

My novel, *Kakemono Hotel*, is a kind of Hitchcock story. It takes place in the dampness of Normandy, in the heart of a sea-side resort: an old lady wills her house to her nephews. The theme: how does one become a criminal without creating difficulties?

The theme of my fourth volume dealing with the elements is, I think, self explanatory — *The Story of the Forest*.

ROBERT SABATIER

INTERVIEWER'S NOTE:

Sabatier's parents died when he was very young; his early
years were difficult, both economically and emotionally.
At the age of twenty (in 1943), he joined the *maquis*.
Later, he founded a small magazine, *Cassette*, and published the poetry of Eluard as well as the verses of
lesser known writers. By 1950 he had moved to Paris
and was haunting literary circles. Encouraged to write
poetry by such notables as Supervielle, Eluard and others,
Sabatier produced *The Solar Feasts (Les Fêtes solaires)*.
His novels include *Sketch on a Sidewalk (Dessin sur un
trottoir)* (1946), *Boulevard, Duck Blood (Canard au Sang)*
(1962), *Safety Matches (Allumettes svédoises)*, *Three
mint-flavored Lollypops (Trois Sucettes a la menthe)*,
etc, the last of which were best sellers.

Q.   Can you tell us about your first novel, *Alain and the
     Negro?*

A.   I was very lonely at the time. I was living in a
     maid's room on the top floor of an apartment building
     in Paris. I really didn't believe in what I was writ-
     ing. In fact, I didn't even send the manuscript to a
     publisher. A friend of mine who read it one evening
     suggested I submit it. I finally agreed and it was
     accepted. That's how I became a novelist.
          I wrote many novels after that — some good,

some bad. But then I began feeling a bit bored with this genre. I returned to poetry, to essays. Suddenly something strange happened to me. I went to New York. It was August and very hot. I was walking on the lower East side — in little Italy. I saw two children open a fire hydrant, the water spurted out and they began playing around in the water and mud. Just as I saw these children, an image burst into mind. I saw myself as a child playing around in my little street in Montmartre. I really don't know whether — as Bachelard said — water is the bearer of souvenirs or not, but when I returned to Paris I felt compelled to write about my childhood. The net result: *Safety Matches*. I gave it to a publisher who read it. He said: "It's like your poems. It's confidential. It won't get very far." I didn't care, I told him. I just want to publish, to be in print. It makes me happy. We were all surprised when *Safety Matches* became a best seller. I was happy from a financial point of view. It permitted me a few of the luxuries of life.

Thereafter, I thought I would write full time. But I experienced a certain conflict at this point. The poet within was offended. I had entered a different category now. I was not pleased really with the fact that I had written a best seller. Solitude had been an indispensable tool for me. It was via solitude that I was able to evolve, to progress as a writer. I no longer enjoyed the loneliness which comes with anonymity and poverty.

Q. You mentioned Gaston Bachelard before. Did you study with him?

A. In a way. We had an unusual relationship. I worked for the University Presses in France, the publisher of Bachelard's works. Bachelard had asked me to supervise the publication of his books. He used to

attend the directors' meetings at the publishing house
and was bored to death by them. Instead of going to
the meetings he would come to my office and we
would spend long hours talking together. Poetry.
Literature. Our conversations were not always
esoteric. Frequently, they broached personal matters,
personal opinions. He enjoyed the writings of
Marguerite Duras, of Marguerite Yourcenar, of Henri
Bosco and others. What interested him in particular
was the use they made of certain images and of the
sensations which emerged from such visualizations.
I think I learned more from these conversations than
any of his students at his Sorbonne lectures.

Q.   You didn't by chance jot down these conversations?

A.   Yes. I did. I have always kept a diary and included
     in it both intimate details and literary events of
     interest to me. I noted Bachelard's conversations
     as well as those of Camus. Camus had always en-
     couraged me, particularly during those years when I
     was a struggling young poet.

Q.   Would you call your novels abstract? or realistic?

A.   Realistic. What is of import to me is the recounting —
     and in the simplest fashion — of what I see and think
     at the time the action in my novels is taking place.
     I trace landscapes, images, perhaps in the style of
     the folklorist who strolls about the countryside
     gathering information concerning costumes, customs,
     etc. There is a social aspect to my novels: the
     period in which the action is situated is described
     in detail.
          Yet, the world of the dream exists in my poetry.
     I underwent a strong Surrealist influence, tempered
     afterward by a kind of search for form.

Q.   Did you know André Breton?

A.   Yes.   But only superficially.   I met him one day on
     Place Blanche.   He used to go there quite frequently
     to meet his Surrealist friends.   I happened to live
     right near Place Blanche at the time.   We spoke
     about Eric Satie.   He told me he had once owned a
     book on Satie before the war but had lost it.   I told
     him I would send him my copy.   We exchanged a few
     letters.   I never knew him well, except through his
     books.   Sometimes we met on Sundays.   He loved to
     go to the Flea Market and so did I.   He was always
     searching for some *realistic* object in the hodge
     podge of the Flea Market.   I was never a member of
     the Surrealist group.

Q.   How do you define Surrealism?

A.   You certainly ask difficult questions... It's an im-
     possible question.   Surrealism implies a kind of life
     which extends beyond the domain of art, poetry...
     beyond the *real*.   It means a revolt against conven-
     tional ideas, well-worn forms... a rejection of the
     bourgeois way of thinking, the banality and stupidity
     of the "Belle Epoque."   Surrealism at its inception
     performed the same function – in 1924 – as the New
     Novelists have performed today.   Both have done
     away with the dust of past ideations, with musty
     ways and clichés.   Both are thrust into new paths,
     new ways...

Q.   The critic R. M. Albérès speaks of the "populism"
     inherent in your novels.   Would you care to elaborate
     on this notion?

A.   I despise the word "populism."   No sooner does a
     writer situate his action **and** a critic comes along
     and labels all of his works.   Just because I have

written about the populace does not mean that my novels always treat the same kind of person. Since I have lived among 'the people,' it is natural for me to describe certain aspects of the environment in which I was brought up. My intention, however, was not to edify or to idealize this group, to analyze the depth of the thoughts of those who congregate at the corner bistro. On the other hand, I have written non-populist novels — *Sketch on a Sidewalk,* for example, which has nothing to do with 'the people.' It takes place in an artistic milieu. *The Chinaman in Africa* describes an aristocratic milieu. *Three Mint-flavored Lillypops* brings to life a bourgeois environment. No one labeled me a "bourgeoisiste" after the publication of *Three Mint-Flavored Lolly-pops.* People love to stamp labels on all writers, to limit them.

Q.   Who were your literary ancestors?

A.   Poets. I studied poetry — that of the Middle Ages, of the Renaissance, eighteenth and nineteenth centuries... Poetry is the high note of literature, as far as I am concerned.

I was also impressed with the works of Dickens, Rabelais and others: Valéry, Supervielle.

I cannot really claim to be the disciple of any one writer. There is something rather undisciplined about me, something which develops alone, in a solitary fashion — far from the crowd. I mean by this that ever since I was a child, I have known loneliness and have profited from such isolation. My education was rather haphazard. A little whimsical. Fanciful. Don't forget, I was the little boy from Montmartre that I described in *Safety Matches.* I am that little boy in *Three Mint-flavored Lollypops* who was brought up in a bourgeois household, who had his studious side. All of this lives within me — blends within me.

Q. You personified Paris. It became a lyrical entity,
the veritable protagonist in *Boulevard* and *Duck
Blood*. How did you manage such a feat?

A. I tried to recreate those fantastic elements which are
intrinsic to the city of Paris. In *Boulevard*, for
example, there is an image of a little boy standing
on a roof top. He's sad. He sees the passersby on
Sunday. He watches them as one observes a flowing
stream. Then, slowly, he comes down, he mingles
with the crowd as one would jump into a river. There
are other picturesque or even picaresque aspects to
the novel.

In *Duck Blood* I wanted to portray certain types
of people. They are out of style today. Paris has
become a sad city, a city where people are constantly
running here and there and nowhere. In the old days,
people used to say that the French were the happiest
people on earth. They had community spirit. It's
no longer a city where contacts may be made and
bonds tightened. I still remember my own childhood
spent in this happy city, at the time flooded with
light and life. A dazzling city, with its own bril-
liance and radiance which I tried to inject in *Safety
Matches*. It's not that I regret my past. But I had
the distinct impression that the Paris of my youth
had disappeared and that people were now uncon-
sciously searching for the *camaraderie* they had
once enjoyed. It may not have been just chance
that made me write *Safety Matches* in 1968. It just
happened that I found myself on the street one day
during the May uprisings. I was convinced that one
of the reasons for these rebellions on the part of
the young was due the fact that they had lost contact
with each other — and themselves. They were fighting
desperately to renew the links, to become part of
some mass movement, some great event. I referred
to the event as a kind of *feast*. Everyone was

moved. Everyone spoke to each other on the street. A fraternity of spirit emerged.

On my little street, on Rue Labat, which was cosmopolitan when I was a child, we used to play outside many hours at a stretch. We used to sit on door steps and talk to our neighbors, to people in general. Streets were not outdoor garages then as they are today. They were the breeding ground of an intense life, gayety, disputes — we participated in the life of the collective, of the people. As Hugo's character Gavroche said in *Les Misérables*: "I entered the street." Now people "enter" their homes. They lock the doors. They sit down in front of their televisions and remain there all night.

Q. Is it the "village" aspect of Paris which you regret?

A. Certainly. *Safety Matches* describes my childhood spent among the people. The second volume deals with my bourgeois years. The third treats my life spent in a rural area. I was sent to Gevaudan to live with my grand parents. There I took care of the cows. I lived a country existence. I experienced the same type of secure feeling that I had known on Rue Labat in Paris. It was certainly the village aspect of my Montmartre street which was most meaningful to me — not the tourist dives.

Q. How do you feel about the New Novelists? the Structuralists? the Imagists?

A. I first came into contact with the New Novelists during a colloquy in Germany. Robbe-Grillet was there. My first reaction was negative. Then I tried to understand what they were attempting. I was shocked at **first**. I could not understand why they rejected characters, psychology . . . . As I grew to appreciate their works I began to admire their will to fantasize, particularly in the novels of Robbe-Grillet. I was fully aware of the fact that I could not rally to their banner. I was an individualist and would have to make my own way.

Other writers wanted to fight the "New Novelists" and wanted me to rally to their banner. I certainly did not join these authors.

It must be noted, however, that even the most conventional writers today were influenced by the theories of the New Novelists. Barthes would probably smile if he heard me say that without the New Novel, I would never have been able to write *Safety Matches* — at least not in the style in which it was written. Yet, nothing really happens in *Safety Matches*. The action: an orphan boy strolls about the streets of Paris. Unlike the New Novel, however, the objects, people and sensations described in my novel are always viewed through the child's eyes — his perceptions. He was the one who interested me. One of the great contributions of the New Novelists made was to rid the literary world of well-worn clichés and of a tired way of seeing life and art.

Q.   Are your novels socially oriented?   Do they pose religious questions?

A.   I'm not interested in religion at all. I am interested in the social aspects of life. When I create characters I project myself onto them, their future and, their environment. I am the child or the adult who is talking. Like Flaubert, who said "I am Madame Bovary," I may say the same thing about my characters.

I am not a social reformer, however.

Implicit in my novels is the meeting of generations: the young and the old, in the manner of a Balzac, in *Safety Matches*; of Alain and the Negro

in the novel of the same name. But implicit in the
blending of generations is the notion of exile. People
have said to me: "How is it that you who were born
in France of French parents, whose roots are so
deeply entrenched in the land, who leads such a
solid life – how is it that you always talk about
exiles, that your characters are always uprooted,
walk along here and there and everywhere." The
protagonist in *The Chinaman from Africa* says: "I
would like to find my place in the world, as a book
does between two volumes." But he does not succeed.

I have not been able to find my own roots. Perhaps because my street, the Rue Labat, was so
cosmopolitan. After the war people from all over
the world congregated on my street: Spaniards,
Russians, Italians, Bretons... It was like a United
Nations, I felt this same bond, this same warm feeling
of unity when I visited small towns in Greece and in
Crete, or in the Auvergne area in France. People
just want to chat with each other, to communicate in
some way.

I have always suffered from a deep sense of
exile, a desire and need to communicate and to be
bound to others. I am an exile in terms of space and
time. I long for the past, for centuries gone by.
Perhaps I was born too late. I am out of step with
my times. I also felt exiled because I was always
alone as a child. My protagonists are frequently
deeply pained because each time they think a link
has been tightened, it suddenly snaps and floats
away.

I wanted to invent characters and place them in
unusual situations, hoping upon hope that they would
be able to discover a way of communicating with
each other and of learning more about themselves. I
write to learn about myself.

Then comes a point when the writer is no longer

responsible for what he writes. His characters take on life and when they do he loses his own identity. Sometimes, when I begin writing a novel, I have a certain protagonist in mind. I decide that he will be the central character. Then, in the course of my labors, I discover that another character is assuming greater importance, that he wants to make his voice heard. I acquiesce to the needs of this secondary character, who then becomes the main one. I am always surprised when I write. I never know what will happen. Writing is a game, a joy, an opening onto the unknown. I love the unknown. I search for it always. When I telephone, for example, and dial the wrong number by mistake, I have the impression of coming up against a void, a mystery. When I try to remember something I had forgotten, a name, I feel as though I am on the threshold of the unknown. We are always seeking the unknown, always going toward it in life, toward the imperceptible. When I write a novel or a poem, I have the impression of coming to grips with mystery.

Q.   Have you thought of writing film scenarios or plays?

A.   No. I'm not made for this kind of writing. Scenarios require a complicated and elaborate story line. I don't feel that I want to do this kind of writing.
     I have always dreamt of writing for the theatre. Perhaps later on. Right now I have a series of novels I want to finish. I began them fifteen years ago. I also want to complete certain essays, poems — hundreds of pages.

Q.   How did you become a member of the Goncourt Academy? What is your opinion of this august literary group?

A.   After the publication of *Safety Matches*, journalists

labeled me the "Poulidor" of literary prizes. Poulidor, you recall, was a runner who was adored by
everyone but who always came in second. That's the
story of my life. My novels — for example, *Blood
Duck*, *Safety Matches* and others — were always placed
on the Goncourt list, but never won a prize. But the
readers of *Safety Matches* enjoyed a kind of revenge,
since this novel sold more copies than any volume
awarded the Goncourt prize.

One day Hervé Bazin asked me to become a
member of the Goncourt Academy. I said "No. I am
against the whole idea of Academies." But then
Bazin spoke to me about the Academy at length.
"We have a lot of old people as members of the
Goncourt Academy. Their ideas differ from ours. We
need to overhaul the Academy, to take in new blood,
to renew it." So I accepted. Then suddenly five
great writers — all over eighty — died. They were replaced by younger writers. Jean Cayrol, for example,
who was elected to the Goncourt Academy to succeed
Alexandre Arnoux. The average age has dropped by
thirty years.

As for literary prizes, I used to be against them.
But they serve a purpose. Publishers are always
looking for financial remuneration. If they feel a
book will win a prize and sell thousands of copies,
then they will print it. That's how so many relatively
unknown writers get their chance. Moreover, reading
is a dying pastime in France today. People just
don't buy books anymore. Only when September
comes around — the prize-awarding time in France — do
people become interested in literature. Newspapers
carry articles and essays; magazines will print ex-
tracts, etc. People buy Goncourt prize novels as
they would a box of candy. Even if they don't read
the volume, it is hoped that someone in their en-
tourage will — eventually.

Many mediocre books have won Goncourt prizes...
but then so have the works of Proust, of Malraux. We
must try in all ways to interest the public in reading.
What greater joy is there than sitting down to a good
book!

RAYMOND QUENEAU

INTERVIEWER'S NOTE:

Raymond Queneau, one of the deans of French letters, is
known for his verbal acrobatics, his prowess in imagery,
and his successful attempts to forge a new language in
his novels, essays and poems. He is the inventor of
words, the destroyer of conventional syntax; but it is
his humor above all and his gift for satire and irony which
have brought him such accolades from the reading public.
Among his numerous volumes, one may mention *Children
of Loam (Enfants du Limon)* (1938), *Pierrot My Friend*
(1942), *Sticks, Numbers and Letters* (1950), *The Sunday
of Life* (1951), *Zazie in the Subway* (1959), etc. Queneau
has been associated with Gallimard since 1938, and is
now the director of the Pléiade Encyclopedia.

Q.   Why did you break with the Surrealists?

A.   I broke with André Breton in 1929. It was a personal
     matter, though there were political ramifications to
     our disagreements.   Breton was going through a
     personal crisis at the time. I don't really want to go
     into our relationship in detail.
          Surrealism *was* Breton. When I speak of Sur-
     realism, I mean the "Breton School." He invented
     everything.   Without him, the word *Surrealism* has
     really no meaning.   But Surrealism today does not
     interest me.   I find it false.   Breton's interest in

automatic writing, for example, seems insignificant to me. He said that the *real movement of thought* could be reproduced via automatic writing. Thought cannot be revealed this way.

I wrote about Surrealism and its "errors" in a series of articles which were published in *The Voyage to Greece*. I also find the *facile* way of writing, which the Surrealists praise, anathema to me. I am against those authors who just pour out one chapter after another, who merely transcribe what emerges from their unconscious without perfecting it, working at it — pruning it!

Q.   When and how did you meet Breton?

A.   I met him after the opening of the Surrealist Center, at the end of 1924. Breton's group met me in the home of a friend of mine, Pierre Naville, the sociologist. It was at Naville's home that I met Breton. Shortly thereafter, in 1925, I began my military service. I was sent to Morocco. When I returned, two years later, we became rather **intimate**. But by 1929 we were at odds.

Q.   Did you know Antonin Artaud?

A.   I corresponded with him when he was interned in the **mental** institution at Rodez. During the German **Occupation** of France I was supposed to visit him, but I got sick and the trip was canceled. Artaud wrote to me during this period. His letters begged me to find a way to have him released from the mental institution, asked me for drugs, books, food, etc. I must say that most of the letters are not very original. Most of them ask for some kind of help.

Q.   Will you publish these letters?

A. I have been asked to do so. There was one letter of interest among the lot. He wrote it before he left for Ireland – in search of St. Patrick. This letter is filled with occult messages and ideations.

Q. Maurice Nadeau has written the following about your work: "Raymond Queneau exalts perpetual invention, the bursting forth of the spoken word, always so close to reality, to the emotional, the visceral." Would you care to comment on this statement?

A. When I wrote my first novels, French writers had really no precise ideas concerning the novel as a rigorous literary genre. They wrote one or two chapters and then proceeded along their own subjective lines. I think technique is most important.

Q. What was the genesis of your novel, *Zazie in the Subway?*

A. The title came to me by chance, about 1945. The word "zazou" meant, at the same time, a kind of hippy. I thought I would write a novel about this type of person – a girl who saw the world only via the metro. But about this same time a child's book was published which featured a little girl who spent her days riding in the subway. So I gave up the idea. But the word "zazou" still intrigued me. I decided to change the name of my heroine to Zazie and dramatize the peregrinations, the antics, and the verbigerations of a seven year old girl. Zazie is a purely imaginary creation. I had no model for her; no little girl in mind. *Zazie* is not a satiric novel.

Q. Do you write your novels quickly? At one or two sittings?

A. That depends. Usually I think about the theme I want

to present for a long period of time. It grows within me; it ferments, so to speak. It has to be this way. I'm so busy at the Gallimard publishing house and I have so many commitments, I just cannot take the time out to spend long months and years on a manuscript. But once the novel or the essay or the poem has taken shape in my mind, I write it out rather rapidly.

Q.   You are also interested in the mathematics of language and are of co-founder of the *Ouvroir de littérature potentielle* (OLP) (*Potential Literary Work-Room*)?

A.   We are searching for new literary forms, new genres, new types of rhetoric. It is a search that locates itself at the confines of mathematics — it is perimathematical. We have around fifteen members who are not only writers but mathematicians as well. OLP is a group effort.

Q.   Is it politically oriented, like *Change* or *Tel Quel*?

A.   No. Though some of our members are also members of *Change*, OLP is an independent and a-political organ. Incidentally, it was founded before *Change* and *Tel Quel*, in 1960. Ours is a truly mathematical literary organ.

Q.   Why are you so drawn to mathematics?

A.   Our mind works just this way. It's hard to pinpoint Claudel once said that literature is very mathematical. One has to "know how to count up to twelve in order to write an alexandrine."

OLP published perimathematical fiction. One of my short stories, for example, is based almost completely on the reader's participation. Each step of the story offers two solutions. The reader chooses one of them, and so on.

Q. You're a Pythagorean?

A. Let's say so. There is an analytical side to our work. For example, I constructed a poem using only the last words of a Mallarmé sonnet. It was very Mallarméan.

Q. Yours is ultra-cerebral writing. It reminds me of the verses of the Medieval Rhétoriqueurs. They constructed poems as one thinks up a puzzle or a mechanical device. They gave little room to the imaginary faculties.

A. Our work has something in common with the literary games indulged in by the Rhétoriqueurs. We consider the Rhétoriqueurs to be our literary ancestors. In fact, one of the members of our group, Albert-Marie Schmidt, who died just a few years ago, was no writer at all, but a professor of literary history. His specialty was the fourteenth and fifteenth centuries.

The Greeks also enjoyed playing on words.

Perec decided some time ago to write a novel without using the letter "e". It was a feat.

We have used all types of literary devices. One such technique consisted in changing nouns in a certain part of the book and replacing them with the seventh which followed each one of them in a dictionary. The results were unbelievable. Since we used all types of dictionaries they took on vastly different flavors.

"A Thousand Billion Poems" is a series of ten sonnets which I wrote using the same rhymes. Each verse is printed on a small sheet of paper. The reader may choose one of the ten possible lines and create his own poem in this manner. There are one thousand billion possibilities in this kind of endeavor.

Q.   Have you used computers to write poems?

A.   Computers have been used to select (at random) some of those thousand billion poems and also to exhibit them.   The inventor of computers, Turing, said: "only a computer can appreciate a poem written by a computer."

Q.   Which of your works is your favorite?

A.   *The Blue Flowers* or *The Sunday of Life*.   I don't really know why.   In *The Blue Flowers*, I focus on a person who goes back in time – and one who emerges from some past era.   In other words, modern and ancient.   My historical character lived in the thirteenth century and reappears every one hundred and seventy-five years until he meets the other protagonist and becomes his contemporary.   There is an old Chinese saying in this connection: "I dream that I am a butterfly and pray there is a butterfly dreaming he is me."   The same thing can be said of the characters in my novel – those who live in the past dream of those who live in the modern era – and those who live in the modern era dream of those who live in the past.

The title of *The Sunday of Life* is a quotation from Hegel.   The character is a kind of homologue of another protagonist – Pierrot.   He is detached from the world which surrounds him.   The action takes place in Paris, shortly before World War II, near the Lyons railroad station.

I am also very fond of *Icarus' Flight*, perhaps because its the last novel I wrote.   It's a historical work; the year is 1895.   A novelist is in the midst of writing his *magnum opus* when he suddenly realizes that his main character has disappeared. He is convinced that he has been stolen. Notice the pun in the French title "Le Vol d'Icare." The word "vol" may mean both "flight" and "theft." This word which is so ambiguous is the pivotal point of the novel.

Q. You mentioned certain characters before — Pierrot, Zazie, Icarus. Do you construct these beings cerebrally, as you do some of your poems, like a computer?

A. I don't know. No. They either exist within me or not. I do not believe I construct them. Nor do I dream them. They lie dormant until they are aroused to action.

Q. What is your opinion of the very modern avant-garde writers?

A. Please, my position with Gallimard prevents me from speaking openly about my contemporaries. But now — let me interview you!

ANDRE PIEYRE DE MANDIARGUES

INTERVIEWER'S NOTE:

Mandiargues was born in Paris in 1909. His father came from the Languedoc region. As a child, his mother was one of Renoir's favorite models. She posed for his celebrated painting, "L'Enfant Blanc." Mandiargues joined the Surrealist group in 1946, after Breton's return to France. Though Mandiargues began writing when he was twenty-six years old he did not publish until World War II. He spent the Occupation years in Monte Carlo with his friends. He is the author of poems, art criticisms, short stories, and novels. Among his best known works are *The Lily of the Sea* (1956), *During the Sordid Years* (1949), *The Black Museum* (1946), *The Motocycle* (1963), *The Margin* (1967), *The Lunar Dial* (1972), etc. He publishes nearly a volume a year.

Q.   Could you explain your ties with the Surrealists?

A.   I have spiritual affinities with the Surrealists – with Miro, Tanguy, Ernst. It's difficult to define Surrealism. André Breton was Surrealism. It was he who gathered the disparate personalities which constituted the corps of Surrealism, and who welded them together. When Breton met young and talented painters or poets, he would encourage them to create. He would inspire them. But, on the other hand, he would also require complete submission and docility

on their part. They would have to yield to his will.
I never did. I was independent.

I was a Surrealist for twenty years. I was less
fanatic than Breton. He was an anarchist, a Trot-
skyite. I am neither a Marxist nor a materialist.
I belong to the extreme Left today.

I wrote *During the Sordid Years* in 1943. It was
my first Surrealist work. Incidentally, I am convinced that Surrealist writers are far more important
than Surrealist painters.

But many of my writings are not Surrealist-
oriented. My styles differ with my moods, my ideas,
according to the inspiration of the moment. I write
short stories, poems and essays; and now I have
written a play, *Isabelle Morra*. The action takes
place in the sixteenth century. It's about a beautiful
poetess who was murdered by her brothers.

Q.   How do you construct your novels?

A.   My novels are very complicated. Each one of them
     takes me from three to four years to write. I note the
     minutest details of the scene which I am describing
     or the place where the action occurs. Like the
     naturalists, Flaubert in particular, I always visit the
     site which I plan to describe in my novel. With
     paper and pencil in hand I jot down all the details
     and in a meticulous manner. Yet, there is a great
     deal of imagination which goes into my work. It's
     not just a copy of nature *per se*.

Q.   Are your themes, characters, or plot lines ever based
     on your dreams?

A.   Yes and no. During the war years (which I spent in
     Monte Carlo, not because I had to but because my
     friends were there), I made great use of my dreams.
     In fact, I must admit I cultivated my dreams. I dis-

ciplined myself in such a way that whenever I dreamed
something of interest, I noted it down. *During the
Sordid Years* is made up of many such dreams. But
then, strangely enough, I went through a kind of
personality change. Before the war I was timid and
introverted. I stuttered. I did not like to be with
people. I am still a rather solitary person. I don't
stroll far from my apartment. In fact, I rarely leave
my apartment unless it is to take a long trip to
Mexico or to Italy. Before the war I was a rather
disagreable fellow. I was neurasthenic. I was
wealthy at the time and did not have to work. I wrote
for my own pleasure. I never showed my manuscripts
to anybody. I was much too timid. After the war,
however, I lost my money and had to earn a living.
I began writing and publishing – out of need. My
stuttering suddenly vanished.

I must admit that I am not in tune with modern
civilization. I detest the mechanics of modern life.
In fact, I never type my manuscripts. I write them
out in long hand, then send them to the publisher
with the proviso they be returned to me intact. Then
I sell the manuscripts.

Q.   You are always drawn to the fantastic in your writings?

A.   Yes. That's why I like French and German Romanti-
cism. That's why I like Balzac. In fact, he is one
of my favorite writers. It's not the realistic side
of Balzac which excites me – his preoccupation with
money or with business affairs. It's his romantic,
occult, and spiritual preoccupations which haunt
me – his fantastic side. I love his descriptions of the
seamy, dark sides of life and his emphasis on love,
crime, blood, night life, etc. *The Duchess of Lang-
eais* had a tremendous influence upon me. I take
my style seriously and that's why I love Balzac and

not a writer like Sartre, for example, whose works
were so lauded after World War II and whose style is
so utterly sloppy.

Q. You were also influenced by Achim von Arnim,
Novalis, Kafka, Sade, and many others?

A. Yes. I was influenced by many writers. I say — and
in all modesty — that I am a cultured person. I have
done a lot of reading. In fact, that is one of the
reasons I began to write. I wanted to feel the same
excitement, the same thrill when writing as I did
when reading. Baudelaire, von Arnim, Kafka, Mallarmé were all important to me, as were others. I
remember a serious disagreement I had with Breton
because he did not like Mallarmé. But after talking
at length with him about this Symbolist poet, I finally
convinced Breton of his greatness, and afterward, of
course, Breton lauded him as he should have at the
outset.

Cervantes also influenced me. I imitated *Don
Quixote* consciously. Johann Richter was also important to me. So were the Spanish and Italian
baroque writers. I appreciated Dickens' darker moods:
his sinister descriptions of men hanging in dismal
halls or alleys, dank and terrifying places which he
alone knew how to portray, characters which grew on
the reader because of their haunting and fearful ways.

Q. Which of your books do you like the best?

A. *The Lily of the Sea* is my happiest novel. The atmosphere is sensual. It's the kind of atmosphere that
existed in the original paradise. The action takes
place in Sardinia. The world which emerges is
voluptuous, magical, hypnotic.

The Motocycle is perhaps the most complex of
my novels. It is constructed via a series of colors,

as are many of my works: in this case, black, white
and red — representing German nationalism, German
cruelty and death. It depicts a mechanical society
which is dangerous and leads or draws one toward
annihilation.

The Margin is constructed around red and yellow
— or Franco's flag. These colors represented blood
and excrement — shit. The novel is built along geo-
metrical lines. Everything in the novel alludes to
the egg which, as you know, symbolizes both life
and death. Life is nurtured within the egg. It is
protected by the shell which preserves the embryo.
If the egg is broken before the time is ripe, the life
enclosed within it perishes. The egg is also an
Orphic symbol and represents the world, the globe.
The Margin is replete with details, brief asides
which at first may seem peripheral to the plot line
but which in fact are intrinsic to it. When writing
The Margin, I made eight trips to Barcelona. I jotted
down every important detail. The novel took me four
years to write.

Some of my short stories are veritable linguistic
exercises. I alternate between prose and poetry.
The tone, the words, and rhythms vary according to
the inspiration of the moment. One of my short
stories was written in the interrogative and so the
reader never really knows whether the events narrated really took place or not. Sometimes my short
stories require great effort on the part of the reader.

Q. The critic Guy Dumur spoke of dédoublement in
your novels: the "two forms of knowledge" — outer
and inner. Do you care to comment on this statement?

A. He is correct. I feel everything in terms of opposites.
It could be said that I have a Manicheistic personality. Manicheism is an old Gnostic sect and is
based on a play or tension of opposites. I see white

and black together; heights and depths. When I look at myself in the mirror I see that both sides of my face are different. I believe in the simultaneity of contraries. I experience extremes in moods. I change positions rapidly. I am a person of extremes – in points of view, in relationships, in all ways.

Q. When you write, you frequently indulge in a series of image associations?

A. Yes, and metaphors also. Not in the manner of a Proust, because I never liked his early works, when he talked about society people, etc. I liked his last volumes, *The Prisoner*, for example, because of the exaggerations. Proust and I have one thing in common – we both like Balzac.

Q. How do you feel about the "New Novelists?"

A. I like Sarraute and Robbe-Grillet. Let's leave it at that. Robbe-Grillet is probably one of the few writers today who really knows how to write. He creates his books and then thinks up his theories. Ricardou is also very talented. I admire his works. I find Le Clézio of great interest. He is a modern mystic. Le Clézio writes for a nonpolitical magazine, *Cahiers du Chemin*, and not for the politically oriented *Tel Quel* or *Change*.

Q. You have written a great deal on modern art. What is your latest volume in this field?

A. I have written a book for the Galerie Maeght on Chagall and one on Miro.

Q. What about the young artists today? Are there any you really admire?

A.   Their art is too facile. An artist must work, strain, anguish in order to create. Today painters think that the easy way is the right way. Art must be difficult. There is a time during the creative process when inspiration should explode — as the Surrealists stated. But after this initial burst of intuition, the artist — like the artisan — must labor.   Facility leads to sterility.   That's one of the reasons I like the new writers like Ricardou.   They at least have made things difficult.

Q.   You said that much of your inspiration was drawn from your dreams. Have you tried drugs?

A.   Many of them. I have taken hallucinogenic drugs, hashish, cocaine, opium, and various kinds of mush-rooms, LSD.   I have never tried peyote, I regret this.   But drugs have little effect on me. I think I rebel against them. I prefer *directed reverie* which leads much further into the domain of the fantastic and the occult than any drug can — at least for me. I have had mystical experiences under the effects of drugs but have gone much more deeply into cosmic spheres and essences under the impetus of directed reverie than via drugs. Though drugs give one acute visions and perceptions, directed reverie delves more deeply into unchartered domains.

     LSD is the most powerful of all drugs. I have taken it several times.   It must be taken in large doses to be effective.

Q.   Doctors maintain that LSD is dangerous, that it dulls the mind, destroys the brain tissue and may even cause schizophrenia.

A.   Rubbish. I don't pay attention to what the doctors say.   It's not good for one's vision, however, par-ticularly if one is old.

But poetry is really the best way of transcending wordly matters — more potent a force than anything else.

Q. You say you are an extreme leftist and that you are close to the revolutionary writers?

A. Yes. Particularly Latin American writers from Chile, Peru, and Mexico. I also admire the Cuban writers. These people are going to change the world. I admire them because they really love humanity and the world *per se*. Their works are dominated by love. They are interested in revolution and in destroying the Anglo-Saxon capitalist regimes which I abhor. America today is far worse than Hitler's Germany ever was. At least Hitler had a Wagnerian vision of the world. America is bent upon destruction. Look at her activities in Asia.   The United States is sordid, criminal, and aggressive as a nation.

Q. Is Russia peace-loving?   What about the lack of freedom of speech in Russia?   Alexander Solzhenitsyn's muzzling. What about the concentration Camps in Russia today.

A. I know many Russian poets who have complete freedom. They can **express** all their ideas. Furthermore, I do not believe in total freedom of speech. I was a Fascist at the outset of my career and a good friend of Ezra Pound, whose ideas I shared.   He was a constant visitor of ours. My wife, in fact, has just **finished** painting his portrait. I adored Ezra Pound. We saw eye to eye on political subjects. There were other great Fascists — the Futurist Marinetti, for example.
I was a-political during World War II. I did not care who won the war. Germany and America represented two forms of evil — each combatting the other.

I believe in absolute liberty, that is, in perpetual explosion, in a volcanic, unstable situation, in perpetual eruption. That's why I liked Pound and that's why I like Castro. They were and are volcanic forces.

Capitalism is dying today. It's falling apart.

Fascism is not as far from Communism as you think. I don't mean Franco's Fascism, but rather Mussolini's Fascism — particularly during the early years of his regime.

ANDREE CHEDID

Andrée Chédid, who is of Egypto-Lebanese origin, was born in Cairo. She is bilingual, for she received her B.A. degree from the American University in Cairo. After moving to Paris in 1946, she became a naturalized French citizen. Since that time she had made brief sojourns in Egypt to see family and friends. Andrée Chédid is the author of novels: *Sleep Delivered* (1952), *The Other* (1969), *The Fertile City* (1973); of plays: *The Numbers* (1968), *Bérénice of Egypt* (1968), *The Showman* (1969); and of poems: *Earth and Poetry* (1956), *Double-Land* (1968), etc.

A product of two civilizations, two ways of life, two psyches, Andrée Chédid's literary works unify the inner and outer aspects of both Occidental and Middle Eastern points of view; they blend disparate notions and ideations into a unity: vast series of images, giant frescoes, visualizations and dramatizations of mysterious and arcane realms.

Q. Did your childhood spent in both Egypt and Lebanon play an important part in your formation as a writer?

A. My childhood was spent largely in Egypt, with frequent trips during the summer months to Europe (to France in particular). I went to school in Paris for three years – from the ages of fourteen to seventeen.

I married when I was twenty-one years old and have two children. I lived in Lebanon only when my husband was in medical school — from 1942 to 1945.

Yes. I believe that one's early years certainly play an important part in a writer's formation. Emotions and images are stamped strongly and indelibly during this formative period. But as far as my writing is concerned, it is less a matter of a nostalgic return to the past, of a concerted search for memories, than it is a need to experience the permanent presence of an inner sentiment — pulsations, movements, chants, misery and joy, sun and serenity, which are inherent to the Middle East. I seem to feel all of these emotions pulsating within me. I believe I was very much marked by both the poverty and the benevolence of those around me. I felt compelled to speak of the simple people in my novels because they seem to be closer to the essentials in life, to the elementary aspects of nature. Of love, death, and of life.

But I always wanted to live in Paris. Perhaps I needed to "uproot" myself or to sever my ties with what I belonged to in order to test or to prove myself. To live outside of one's milieu in an anonymous manner serves to decant, to liberate one. The question of folklore also arises in writing — the area in which the action takes place in the novel — but this is not what I strive for. In addition to the locus, there is a certain *voice* which emerges from the depths of the Middle East and which probably lives within each one of us; that's what I search for. In poetry it is different. One is free of time and place. As far as I am concerned, poetry has no geographical boundaries. It belongs to all lands.

I must say from the very outset that the similarities — not the differences — between beings and civilizations are what fascinate me: the bridges, the junctures, the meeting places (so difficult to touch, to describe explicitly, but which exist, alive, some place within us) which unify, which conciliate.

There are areas where the Occident and the Middle East come to terms, realize that they are each facets of the same reality. One fulfills the other, enriches the other with its own particularities, sounds the other out. It is a dialogue between man.

Q.   Can you explain the themes, images, and symbols of your novel, *The Other?*

A.   The themes in all of my novels are always double. Facts and the myth. On one level, the theme may be understood as a kind of tale, an anecdote. In *The Other,* an old man — despite all odds — is determined to save the life of a young foreigner, the victim of an earthquake. He is convinced that the young man is still alive under the rubble. The old peasant is obdurate. He continues his search. Finally, the young man surges forth from the bowels of the earth.

On another level, the subject revolves around one man's emergence from obscurity, his terrible — but always possible — combat with the forces of darkness, if faith and life are still potent forces within an individual. The old man's simple vocabulary, the extreme attention with which he attends to his task, his fraternity, enables him to construct, little by little, the passage which leads from the shadows to light — for the Other.

This death, this renaissance is implicit in each individual. Everyone bears the seed of his own destruction as well as his own phoenix. Ascension, the fall, and a new ascension... A poem, a book, all forms of expression are born from a desire, a will to emerge, to escape from one's skin, to go toward .... something. I don't know what that something is .... But just to go!..

The question of ''communication'' is also ever present in this novel. The desire each individual

has to connect as well as to disconnect with the
world within and without. At times a glance, a word
suffices — then suddenly, all barriers are broken; all
distances are breached; even the weight of the earth.
There is a *moving* force in poetry, in the desire for
expression. If the machine itself is used properly
it may even become a beneficial agent, a gift, a
privilege (in this novel I am alluding to a wire with
two receivers on either side which serves as a link
for men, etc.)

Q.   Are your characters based on real people? or are
they strictly imaginary?

A.   My characters are always imaginary. I have never
described anyone I have known. Nor have I ever
related a souvenir. My protagonists are amalgams
or blendings of memories and imagination but are
never enclosed or limited in one enclosed area or
another.
       My characters do not really emerge from my
dreams either. I see them as flesh and blood entities.
I want them to be flesh and blood. Materializations
of the unconscious? Perhaps... Perhaps... But
I am searching for an objective view (passionate,
but objective... are these reconcilable?) I haven't
the slightest desire to write about myself or about
my fantasies (perhaps I do anyway, it's up to you to
judge). A character interests me for itself. It is
the "breath within him" which haunts me, which
seems to overflow, whatever its roots, its origins.
       I try to portray characters who live in both a
rooted and uprooted state. They are rooted so they
can become incarnated, so that their joy as well as
their suffering becomes palpable. They are uprooted
entities because they must be rid of any overly
limited or specific personality or nature and become
common sharing to all men — brothers of each one of
us.

I believe, moreover, that what is fundamental to man is the fact that he is both *kneaded* from reality and from irreality. It is for this reason that poetry (even if we are unconscious of it) lives within us — is part of us.

Q. Have you been influenced by one writer in particular?

A. I don't believe I was ever strongly influenced by one writer alone. My memory is flagrantly poor. This may be the reason for this lack of influence. I have always read in a haphazard manner. And then, when I write, for example, I find it difficult to read anything at all — only the newspaper.

　　When I was young I enjoyed the Russian novelists: Dostoyevsky's *The Idiot*, in particular. I also read Shelley, Keats, Shakespeare, Greek theatre, Rimbaud. Modern poetry. When I began writing poetry at the age of twenty or thereabouts I knew nothing about modern poetry. I had not even read the Surrealists.

Q. How did you integrate the sensual and aesthetic elements in your novel, *The Fertile City*?

A. I didn't try to integrate them. It happened by itself. I always correct or touch up my manuscripts, but only after the first flow of words has been set down on paper. I never interrupt the momentum or flow of inspiration. My first version is absolutely illegible, lava. But I find my way in this labyrinth. I cut, I mark out alleys and passages; I change; I alter; I prune. In a way I need this kind of muddy, dank matter in order to compose, to erect, to choose, to reject....

Q. How did you come to write novels, poetry and plays? Can you tell us the differences involved in terms of your creative method?

A.   I began by writing poems. My first volume of verse was published in Egypt and was written in English. For the next ten years or thereabouts I wrote only poetry. Then, short stories. I guess I needed to understand the meaning of human warmth, to express what transcends the individual, what overflows into mankind. But it is always in terms of the simplest and most elemental of individuals that the heart is laid bare.

The work involved in writing short stories is precise and concise. In this respect it is close to poetry. Novel writing is more difficult. At least for me. It is more talkative. But what attracts me to this form of expression is the fact that one must *push* still further, search for the voice, the meaning of life itself; the fact that sensations and beings must be brought to life.

I had always thought about writing plays. When I worked with amateur groups I found the theatre to be an extraordinary place. I realized that play-writing is one of the most perilous types of expression and that great maturity is needed to succeed in this medium. Language has to be ground out. But then there is the joy of feeling and observing the actual incarnation of the word on stage; to be able to assist, perhaps to participate in group work.... Writing is a solitary art. Solitude is necessary. Writing is the work of an artisan — it is a trade, one based on words. One must struggle with the blank page. But then one also needs the others! The theatre gives one companionship.

Much can be said of the various genres. In terms of my own work, poetry dominates everything else. I always return to poetry — as though it were the essential spring. But other forms of expression also fascinate me. Television. Radio. Even a computer. Why not?... But life is too short!

Q.   How do you feel about the "New Novel" which is

really not 'new' today?

A. The "New Novel" performed a function. It forced the novel out of its conventional, habitual and well-worn path.

   Everything that is new is useful and healthy. It frees; it liberates. If one merely follows past literary trends one is caught in a trap. Literature then becomes ossified; it stagnates. But, on the other hand, one must also liberate oneself from the new (when it, in turn, becomes overly formalized). One must free oneself again ... and again ... It is a continual process.

   Art grows in terms of a succession of breaks, perhaps.

   But personally, my taste does not run along the same lines as the theories expressed by the New Novelists. I don't write as they do (though I admire the works of Sarraute, Duras, Simon, Robbe-Grillet and others). Emotion is essential to me. I am not an intellectual, cerebrally oriented. I search for a more direct language. I want to suggest movement from within; the breath (how can one express such a feeling?) as if it were forced to emerge, but through suggestion rather than via analysis.

Q. Can you tell us something about your present work?

A. I have just finished writing a long poem on a single theme: the birth of man and his acceptance of the world. The unbelievable, terrible, and marvelous feelings which surround the mystery of incarnation. It's called *In the Flesh* (Prendre Corps).

   D. H. Lawrence once wrote: "We should dance with rapture that we should be alive, and in the flesh and part of the living incarnate cosmos."

   I am also writing a novel. The action takes

place in antiquity. Time melts, it blends and fuses in an attempt to discover the cry within all mankind — the moving force to bring the eternal present to life.

I also plan to write more plays. The theatre means freedom to me. Immense possibilities for the creation of a theatrical spectacle which would integrate all disparate elements, but in which language would be maintained.

Q. Michel Bourgeois wrote in *La Quinzaine littéraire*, (December 16-31, 1972) that you practised "the most extravagant type of anarchronism...." Would you care to comment on this statement?

A. I like his use of the word "anachronism." It implies an overlapping of time, the maintaining of an eternal quest, of humanity. The character, Alefa, in *The Fertile City*, is an attempt to fuse time and people. She lives in the Paris of today which she loves and, at the same time, is "elsewhere," everywhere. Rooted and uprooted at the same time.

I sometimes have the impression that as we live our individual existences we come to know so little of ourselves. And that perhaps a simple answer lies within each one of us and within our reach; a place where each one can breathe in peace.

JOSEPH KESSEL

INTERVIEWER'S NOTE:

Joseph Kessel was born on February 10, 1898, in Clara, Argentina. He studied there during his early years but completed his education in France at the Lycée Louis-le-Grand, the Faculté des lettres de Paris and the National Conservatory for Dramatic Arts. He volunteered for the French Air Force in 1917, saw action, and later was sent on a mission which took him to the United States, the Pacific, and Asia. He returned to France in 1919, where he began a career as a journalist for the *Figaro*, the *Journal des Débats*, *Matin*, *Paris-Soir*, reporting from Palestine, the Red Sea area, Spain, Berlin, etc. Kessel was awarded the Croix de Guerre (1914-1918) and the military medal (1939-1945). He is Commander of the Legion of Honor, and was elected to the French Academy in 1962.

Journalist, novelist *(The Crew, The Pure in Heart, Belle de jour, Mermoz, The Rose Laurels,* etc.), and scenario writer *(The Grand Balcony, A Wall in Jerusalem, The Parisian Song,* etc.)

Q.   Would you call your first novel, *The Crew (L'Equipage),* a realistic work?

A.   Yes.   I owe my first novel to a real experience – a great experience: the time I spent at the front with my squadron in World War I, during my nineteenth and and twentieth years. This experience was so moving that I had to tell it. It had to emerge from me. The section of *The Crew* based on documentation is factual. It is so true in fact that some of my friends recognize themselves as people and as participants in the incidents described. The plot, however, is a figment of my imagination.

Q.   Do you have any theories concerning the structure of the novel? Everyone today seems to want to revise, rework or recreate the novel form.

A.   No. I have no theories whatsoever about the structure of the novel. I merely follow my own instincts.

Q.   Who were the writers who influenced you most profoundly?

A.   Tolstoi, Dostoyevsky, Kipling, and Alexander Dumas.

Q.   Which of your novels do you like the best?

A.   A four-volume, cyclical novel, *The Round of Misfortune*; the introduction to volume I, *The Medici Fountain*. I started writing this tetralogy when I was thirty years old and finished it when I was over fifty. Since I was so taken with this project and it obsessed me for so many years — something which is quite contrary to my nature — it must have responded to an inner necessity. Yet, this tetralogy is not a "disguised" biography in any sense of the word. It is an "amalgam of souvenirs, of transferences and of pure fiction . . . ." What I depicted in this novel were the "excesses of a period, of a society, a generation which today passes for being a happy one. But in those days one envied the 1890's . . . ."

Q. André Billy wrote the following about your novel, *The Lion:* "It is written with both a light and vigorous touch. It is realistic and poetic. It was perhaps really lived, and perhaps it was only a dream. It is certainly a very beautiful, pure and original work." Was *The Lion* a dream?

A. Partially. *The Lion* was both lived and it was also the outcome of a dream. I spent a rather long time on a reservation at Amboselli — and under very favorable conditions. The documents in this volume are authentic, as they were for *The Crew*, but the story about the little girl and the lion is, if not completely invented (it stems from an adventure which took place long before my sojourn at the reservation), at least partially so. I think that the entire volume was inspired by my very deep fascination with wild beasts. I have always felt some kind of a huanting affinity with them.

Q. I heard that you were in charge of a series of articles on the State of Israel for the magazine, *Miroir de l'Histoire?*

A. No. I am the editor of the magazine. My task is to find writers to write and not to write myself. I simply wrote a kind of preface to the **first** number in which I explained why I began the series with the story of the Resistance in the Warsaw Ghetto and why this event is unique in history:

> When and where in the history of the world has one seen 500,000 human beings huddled together in a small area, behind a merciless wall, without any real food, without heat, without medicines, suffering from the pangs of hunger, half naked under their rags, freezing; devoured by the flees

of typhus, serving as material and game
for professional torturers, possessed
sadists? This is, nevertheless, how the
Jewish population of the Warsaw Ghetto
lived for four years. They agonized....

FRANÇOISE MALLET-JORIS

INTERVIEWER'S NOTE:

Françoise Mallet-Joris was born in Antwerp on July 6, 1930. Fluent in both French and Flemish, she received the equivalent of a French baccalaureate degree in Brussels, and from 1946 to 1947 traveled in the United States essentially to perfect her English. In Paris once again, she set to work on a Master's Degree awarded to her by the Sorbonne; her field was English and Comparative Literature. She is the mother of four children from the ages of thirteen to twenty-five.

Madame Mallet-Joris' first literary production at the age of fifteen was a volume of verse: *Sunday Poem*. Her novels, *The Beguines' Rampart (Le Rempart des Béguines)* (1951), *The Red Room (La Chambre rouge)* (1955), *The Lies (Les Mensonges)* (1956), *The Celestial Empire (L'Empire céleste)* (1958), *The Tunnel Game (Le jeu du souterrain)* (1973) have won several prizes: the Librarians' Award, the Femina Prize, and the Monaco Prize.

Q. Can you recall what novelists really excited you during your formative years?

A. I used to read many novels — and passionately. I did have a predilection at the outset for German and Russian novelists — Thomas Mann, Dostoyevski, Pushkin — and for Rilke's poetry.

Q.   The critics on the whole asserted that your first
     novel, *The Beguines' Rampart*, shocked your readers;
     that your second work, *The Red Room*, earned its
     success because of the scandalous things in it.
     What is your reaction to such statements?

A.   My first and second novels form an *ensemble*. The
     subject of these two works focuses on the evolution
     of an adolescent. Despite the fact that the critics
     wrote many articles about my novels, these did not
     earn the same commerical success that Françoise
     Sagan's works had.
          My youth, perhaps, inspired me to dramatize a
     subject which was especially close to me. I wanted
     to underline and exteriorize the conflict experienced
     by a child when confronting the adult world. My
     heroine, Helen, at the outset of the novel is a young
     girl with a passion for the absolute. Because her
     imagination is so fertile, Tamara, the novel's other
     heroine, takes on mythical attributes and emerges in
     Helen's mind's eye as a full blown poetic creation.
     When she finally comes to realize that her friend is
     nothing but a human being like others, with the same
     weaknesses and the same concessionary attitudes,
     she hardens and becomes incapable of experiencing
     the sincere love offered to her by a man.

Q.   According to Emile Henriot, *The Lies* is an "admi-
     rable book." Can you discuss its themes?

A.   *The Lies* takes up, at least in part, but conversely,
     the theme of *The Rampart*. We are again faced with
     the problem of an adolescent confronting an adult's
     reality: this time it's on a social level. Thanks to
     the heroine's exceptional integrity, she is in no way
     embittered by her reality and though she sacrifices
     her interests and even her affections, her original

purity is conserved.

Q.   You also take up the question of appearance and
     reality in your novels, as had Nathalie Sarraute,
     Marguerite Duras and Simone de Beauvoir.   Can you
     tell us your views on this subject?

A.   My understanding of appearance and reality focuses
     on a kind of social 'deformation' which most people
     define as an adult attitude and which is, in fact, too
     frequently merely a confused view of certain values.
     My intentions as a novelist is not to analyze this
     problem from a philosophical, political or ideological
     viewpoint. I see it in terms of a theological climate
     based on hope: one makes a sort of bet – to see
     beyond the masks worn by individuals, to peer into
     into an inner reality.

Q.   In what way do you feel your novels have evolved?

A.   Most specifically in terms of their technical structure.
     To break with the classical 'romanesque' novels and
     all they represent (chronological and linear time
     sequences, well-made plots, etc.) and to concentrate
     on the most fragmentary of visions, so deeply nuanced
     by the power of imagination and souvenir, is my goal.
     The secret bond that gradually unites those privileged
     moments finally replaces the artificially created
     links of the classical novel.   The isolation I ex-
     perience during these moments of revelation (or
     creativity) compels me to render the descriptions I
     include in my novels still more precise and to focus
     my attention exclusively on the more revealing
     fragments of a dialogue or inner monologue.   *The
     Tunnel Game* expresses the technical changes my
     novels have undergone most accurately. The passage,
     for example, from one person to another, from one

"intrigue" to another, is accomplished via inner similitudes which may be detected only with the help of the thought process. The bond that exists between the hero who seeks to write a book, attempting all the while to understand the meaning of the gratuity of life, and the one who searches for and finds the treasure, using the evidence at hand, and who experiences his riches in an almost mystical manner, is obvious. The protagonists who gravitate around the two heroes are more or less preoccupied with the same problems.

Q.   What are your plans?

A.   I am working on a novel in which I shall broach the problem of a woman and the complexities of her situation in our epoch.

JEAN-PIERRE FAYE

INTERVIEWER'S NOTE:

Jean-Pierre Faye is avant-garde in his literary concepts.
Author of *Between the Streets (Entre les rues) (1958),
The Break (La Cassure) (1961), Analogues (1964), The
Lock (L'Ecluse) (1964), The Trojans (1970), Iskra (1972),*
etc., he belongs, chronologically speaking, to the Robbe-
Grillet and Butor generation. Yet his contributions go
beyond their innovations. Faye's novels consist of dialogues, monologues, equations, and objects existing
simultaneously on a variety of levels, and narrators whose
natures are ambiguous and who experience life as a series
of reflections. What is of import to Faye is the structure
of the novel as well as the poetic, mythological, spiritual,
terrestrial, spatial, visual, sonorous dramas which emerge
in the actual writing of the work.

Faye is part of the collective, *Change.* The collective, which includes Philippe Boyer, Yves Buin, Jean-
Claude Montel, Léon Robel, and Jacques Roubaud, prints
a magazine three times a year. The first issue was published in 1968 and includes articles on poetry, linguistics,
literary theory, psychological research, "generative
criticism" and, of course, "Rabelaisian laughter." Notables such as Jakobson, Chomsky, Yavin, Klossowski
have contributed their efforts to make *Change* a successful
endeavor.

Q. What was your background? How were you "formed?"

A. Nothing "forms" us, or to put it another way, it's what deforms us that forms us. In other words, what teaches us to see transformations.

   To have listened to and experienced Bachelard and Lévi-Strauss when I was a student, must have helped me change in that way, as much as watching Roger Blin or Jean-Marie Serreau in their daily activity of staging a play. Working on philosophical texts or analyzing economic problems means a lot if it lends to the acquisition of greater transparency of vision. And I would have given everything to have been Blin's or Serreau's assistant, or to have played the role of Edgar up to "burst smilingly" in *King Lear.*

Q. You were first a poet. How and why did you choose the novel to express yourself? What role does poetry play in the structure of the novel?

A. Poetry? the novel? Or rather: prosodiacal power, narrative power? Both are a question of desire.

   First comes the desire for things. You can mold language *around* them. Or displace it *with* them. To mold or to displace; such is language's dual power. Which is the most direct? "Poetry," because it molds language around the things themselves: their shape, their contour. "Narrative," because it grasps relationships between things by displacing itself *along* with them. That is why the first language was a prosodiacal narrative—an epose.

   Then, the gap separating narrative and poetry (or prosody) becomes even larger. Since "Lancelot in prose," the word *novel* has been associated with a narration without prosody. The "anti-Novel" of Charles Sorel—that is to say, the realistic novel—attempts to be most particularly anti-poetic. In Mal-

larmé's "Un coup de dés," the culminating point of
Occidental poetry, "everything becomes a question
of hypothesis: the narrative is avoided."

But the function of prosody is not to be considered as an ornament added to language. It belongs
to it; it is fundamental to it. It acts like a boomerang
of phonic figures on syntax, and, in terms of meaning,
of surface structures on deep structures. It enables
signs to be felt; it uncovers movement in their depths.
It shifts syntax along with a shifting desire, it propels
language around certain points – objects. This is
what effects language in a language.

So there is "poetry" within the narrative – power
itself which acts – the *black power* of language,
desire in language. In both senses of the French
word *langue: language* and *tongue*. What binds
language, what penetrates from mouth to mouth and
from lip to lip.

Q. What does Verdier represent in your first novel,
Between the Streets? Is he a man in search of something?

A. Verdier is the name of the narrator. This is fundamental;" every narrator bears a *name.* If deprived
of a name, which he both bears and carries with him,
a narrative may have a good chance of becoming just
a piece of rhetoric (this is obvious right now in
France – with this group that an American periodical,
Semiotica, has referred to as the Neo-Rhetorical
School.) The name refers to a mouth, to a corporeal
tongue: the narrative's sex. Verdier is a name.
But it belongs to a narrator who does not narrate.
He explores a narrative, he brings objects, names.
Names of women: Mona, Kathleen, Lyn. He is a
"reporter" without knowing it. He is a narrator in
spite of himself and his vision, his language *cuts,*

so to speak, *beneath* the narrative.

You know that the first meaning of the French and English words, *narration, narrative* is the power of knowing: *gnoscens, gnarus, narus*, it's the same word (and also: *knowing*). To penetrate the enigma of the narrative is to explore the power of knowledge at its very source and to introduce oneself to the cerebral network of knowledge. But suppose this network were cut off or disconnected in its very flesh, its meat. (In some way comparable to a lobotomy practised by psychosurgeons, but harshly contested by psychoanalysts.)

Such is Verdier. The narrative which has been separated from itself explores the distances from itself. Desire possesses its object but does not feel its possession. Desire searches for its object but does not know (does not tell) of its pursuit. The frenzy pursuing Mona is in-difference: the equality of narration. (Mona in erotic Venetian slang during the baroque period meant the woman's sex organ, her vulva.)

It's her dangerous indifference: the fact that she does not tell us in advance which of her *traits* will come to menace us, which one is different and significant, which one may be death-dealing.

Q.   Does *The Break* imply a marital, psychological or political break, or does it constitute the novel's form or structure?

A.   A break (in French, *cassure*) means a break in schizophrenia. If the cut in a lobotomy ejects consciousness, separating it from its "innerness," the cut of schizophrenia holds it "within," in its limitless negativity; an inner desert voyage, intensive adventure into nowhere, severed from all "contact with life" and at the same time, "near the throbbing heart of reality'' (G. Deleuze). Where is it?

Can we locate it? Was it initially in the woman, Guiza? But an American critic saw it first in the man as well, in Roncal. Was it *between* the two, within that spatial area of desire enveloping both of them, in the fantasm of this dual group? In the social soil: in the breach within the city, the *polis*, the political relationship mangled by the most oppressive fantasms — those of a colonial imperialist war: the war in Algeria. Haunted by the violent fantasm of torture (Buci Place in Paris, where the carcan punishment took place). Laceration similar to the one which encircles the collective dance: around the hole in which the animal-king is dismembered — this is where killing is effectuated.

Vertiginous holes are dug into space here: caged stairwells, inner courts, giant cracks, crevices and fissures. The narration of these fissures describes itself in the fundamental fissure within the narration, producing this concentric space around itself, this eighth rung space. It now is this very desire which cuts: orgasm, orgy.

Q.   Does the protagonist V in *Beating* (*Battement*) (1962) feel lonely, a stranger in the world and to himself? How important is the anedote in the structure of this novel? Could you describe the themes, the rhythms, the visual and sound effects which you have tried to bring out in this novel?

A.   V is the throbbing of the narrative, its primary prosody, lancinating. It is also the throbbing of desire; but it is also that of pain.

You can say nothing (live nothing) without this double narrative: the ''moi'' which narrates (in the ''imperfect''), the ''lui'' (in the present) which narrates — ''je'' and ''il'' share every measure of the recitative. The city is subject to this permanent pulsation within the blood of language – its "pronominal" blood, which links it to the living corpus which advances, speaks, desires, and produces love.

What V wants – the woman, women who come and go – are the motivating forces of this language, this oscillation which envelops the world, the streets, the city. This city, at one time peaceful, more than any other, now a city of murder, clandestinely divided by a war which is totally foreign to it: Munich, between the insurgent forces on the *Front* ("Forehad") and the fascists on the *Main* ("Hand"). A body secretly dismembered by these fantasms.

And you see how this narrative recaptured prosody, lost since the disappearance of epic works. Pronominal prosody, *syntactic prosody,* which far from "ornamenting" the narration, engenders it.

Q.   What is your conception of time?

A.   Time is *nothing.* What exists is the stamp of time.

Time ripens within me, even when sleeping, but then I dream: I don't know time. As I awaken, I draw or *write* time on space – on material space or on mental space, on the imaginary or on things. When turning around, I grab time through that latticework of space: I narrate it.

The time used in dreaming is interwoven into the time I *spend* writing: the unconscious time of desire.

The same thing can be said of society. One can recover generalized time only in terms of its own space: by seizing its networks of action that act upon one another, in terms of relationships (of narrations) each has with the other. Yet, this time swells, accumulates its machines (including its "time taking" machines), weaves this blind memory beneath the story, made up of stones and metals, and dispersed carbons.

— Proust's social time is no longer valid. It's no longer a suburb which slowly dissolves into a city, like a clepsydra, or a biscuit melting in some tea. It is a world-wide link which grows; where all the knots pull on each other at the same time, where, open-eyes, dreams the desire for death.

It is a question of writing this link, or interweaving it.

Q. Are your protagonists *engagés*? What are their relationships with society? With themselves?

A. Protagonists? Those who act, as Khlebnikov would say: *actants* — acting first, bearers of a primary or immediate narration. First messengers.

These narrators *report* their narration, even when isolated in a boarding house or a foreign language. Language is always the guarantee pledged for involvement. And they always report it *to this area* of general language which is the City, the "polis," the political center, the crossroads where narrations meet.

This is the narrative: a political relationship at its inception, the slow or lightning diffusion of action by means of slow or brief narrations; a chain made up of interlocking notions of desire and death instincts. This is what fiction explores.

That is why the quarrel between "committed literature" and "the New Novel" was anachronistic, and not a pertinent conflict. To be able to rediscover the deepest network, the original chain of active narrations, is to see the death — life relationships involved in the city. But the one to best observe the *passage* of narratives is the "unbiased" narrator.

Q. Do coincidences, the fortuitous, have a function in
    the structure of your novels?

A. Chance? the fortuitous? This is the point at which
    distinct links are severed, where divergencies mo-
    mentarily meet, where infinite *series* brusquely con-
    verge.

    It is exactly at this point that language acts,
    and that gesture is language. And, as with a lapsus,
    that the black weft is suddenly unveiled.

Q. You discuss your conception of the narrative in
    "Hors-Texte" (*An Autocritical Récit*). Would you
    like to explain your ideas in terms of this work?

A. An "Hors-Texte" had to show, for once — but within
    the framework of the plot, with the precision of a
    magnifying glass — how material is woven. The
    construction of lattice-work.

    We do not tell everything. Any more than music
    sounds all of its tones. Curiously enough, the
    lattice-work within the Occidental narrative — under
    the name of "novel" — has, so to speak, accompanied
    that of polyphony. The first mentioned is sister to
    the "Ars Antica;" and the first realistic novel — *Don
    Quixote* and the *Francion* of Sorel, theorized in his
    Anti-Novel ("Anti-Roman") — accompanies the break
    modal music and modern tonality. And just as
    tonality, so called natural harmony, integrated the
    modes of ancient Greek and Asiatic music, so, in an
    analogous manner, did the classical narrative, the
    great Occidental novel, from Cervantes to Balzac to
    Tolstoi, seek to harmonize the elementary narrative
    modes.

    But there is an arbitrary choice in terms of the
    series, behind this "natural" (or naturalist) con-
    struction. The "Lancelot in prose" shows naively

that *between* such and such characteristics in terms of the narrative, there is "nothing to remind us of a tale." Francion is delighted to discover that all else is tellable.

Exception: a narrative series is not a musical series. If a sound is repeated it remains the same sound. A trait, in terms of the narrative, once repeated, is no longer the same; it is hardly analogous. The first narration effects the second one. This network of action, this series of narratives, this *group* of series — these cause the operation of our "complete and true story," so to speak, as the good Francion would say. The simplest of these groups (in the algebraic sense) being the "group of four" — the analogia, as the Greeks called it.

With *Between the Streets, The Break, Beating,* the fourth proportionally, or the "fourth analogously," is *Analogues.* A group of women's narratives strikes the men's narratives, laterally.

The lattice-work — the unveiling of the lattice-work — "is a terrible moment for sensibility" (Artaud). It is the very matter of language.

Q. Is there a relationship between your conception of music (spatial) and that described by Hermann Hesse in *Magister Ludi?*

A. Spatial music: it catches and outlines changes in states.

Groups of "values," in terms of the variety of meanings of this strange word: musical, pictorial, economic, linguistic, algebraic. *Lines* of values — that is, in ancient poetry, verse, the "music of verse." Columns of values (similar to those on the stock **exchange** money exchange...). Matrix of these lines and columns. Matrices bending around their diagonals, becoming a transformation or transmutation of the other....

I would like to show you that *new prosody*, which embraces both "poetry" and the "narrative," is this matrix-like and *pliable* kind of prosody, which envelops us from all directions — in colors, sounds, languages, signs of all kinds striking us at each instant with their stamp. Hammering at us and making for our story.

It is with this element that we play or which plays with us: master of the game or mistress of the sport.

Q.   What role does sickness play in *The Lock?* Is there an evolution in the theme of sickness in your novels?

A.   Sickness does not begin with *The Lock.* It is, rather, a series of tide-gates. (It already finds itself in a strange triangle: lobotomy, schizophrenia, neuralgia). Especially since it's located in the very heart of the divided city, scarred because of a cerebral gash, a cleavage, a pain. Divided by the diagonal of death.

(A double diagonal: Berlin: Jersualem)

But another bearer of illness emerges obliquely. Virgula, and an alteration of blood. The break in the chains of celluler codes, in the "double helix,"* in the folded helix.

Q.   Did you create a mystique of language in *The Trojans?*

A.   Not a mystique of language. Rather the unfolding of language which envelops us, *the machinery of language* which speaks to us and inscribes itself in us. The machinery of cities which writes and speaks the history of the world. The machine capable of exploding a kind of generalized and simultaneous translation of all languages.

*In the sense of J. D. Watson.

The machine of cities — Chicago, Paris, Munich, Basel, Berlin and Troyes (or Troy: first city in the narrative).

But also the machine capable of *encircling the cities* with the "countrysides of the world," with the black weft of a general insurrection against cities, a general propagation of narrations in all directions and in all languages, via the great leukemia of language, the sudden destruction and jamming of all the directive devices on all roads.

Lé Lin (Lin like Lin Piao: before the enigmatic messenger) or the quartering of codes, and the laceration of the black weft (and plot) in the very web of desire, hunger and upheaval.

Q. Would you tell us in detail why you broke with the group known as Tel Quel?

A. Because Tel Quel "changes" with the Styles, the Seasons — the *Fads.* Nevertheless, I really don't like answering this question.

At the beginning, my political, theoretical and literary position was the exact opposite of that held by the group Tel Quel. Tel Quel made its first appearance at the end of 1958 after the May 13, 1958 rightists' *coup d'état,* fomented and executed by the most fanatical supporters of "French Algeria." The first referendum in the autumn of 1958 had proven to be a cruel defeat for the French leftists, the anti-colonialist Left. The earliest political position of the *Tel Quel* group was enunciated in the "Journal" of one of its members at the time — *with the enthusiastic* approval of the "yes" faction of May 13, 1958.** This opinion was openly shared by the

**The movement and uprising in the French Army of Algeria, which brought DeGaulle back into power.

whole group (except for Jean Thibaudeau, who at the
same time, belonged, politically speaking, to the
Editions de Minuit). Huguenin, who during this same
period attacked me violently in *Arts*, later severed
relations with Tel Quel, but for literary reasons — the
New Novel: the question of political dissension
between them never arose. One of their future supporters said: "since May 13, 1958, ushers in the
Second Empire, we must also have a Parnasse...."
Such were the politico-aesthetics of the group during
its months of gestation and its early years. Mauriac
added as a conclusion to a passage in his *Bloc
Notes*, which launched the name Sollers — and this
meant a lot to him, despite his conservative atavism,
as Mauriac was then vehemently opposed to war and
the practice of torture as carried out by the French
army: "I fear that no injustice will distract him from
himself...."

When the first number of *Tel Quel* was finally
published, it was preceded by an unsigned *Declaration* — written by Sollers — in which we read: "Ide-
ologists have ruled long enough over expression....
It's about time a parting of the ways take place,
let us be permitted to focus upon (expression) itself."
At a time when "expression," freed from "political
and moral directives," chose to take care of itself
alone, the French army was busying itself by occu-
pying Algeria, killing a million people and torturing
thousands of others.

Let's skip the details concerning this period.
It was during this period that French writers and
intellectuals regrouped and supported the manifestos
written by Blanchot and Merleau-Ponty against
colonial war. The only ones able to escape from
this anti-fascist movement were the writers of the
Nimier-Blandin-Perret group (the "Hussards," the
"Droite Buissonnière) and the Sollers-Boisrouvray-

Hallier group — the Tel Quel Group. The latter group
has just rendered political homage to Céline — in *Tel
Quel* and in *L'Herne*, by comparing him to Sade. My
position concerning this view point has been expressed in a note which was published in *Esprit*, entitled:
''To Sade's rescue . . . .''

The limit of this involvement with the rightists
under the guise of traditional Apolitism (we all know
that the Right is ''apolitical)'' . . . was reached when
this group rallied to the aesthetic and literary banner
of the Editions de Minuit and the Nouveau Roman.
(He forgot to say that the great writers of the New
Novel supported the great anti-colonial manifestos
at this time . . . .)   But let's overlook this detail.
Because Sollers sided with this group he protested
the attempted murder of Jérome Lindon in his home.
Our first meeting resulted from protest. A year after
the end of the Algerian war, the group informed me
that it had co-opted me.   This co-option was announced in the magazine *Arts* — before I had even
actually accepted it.   I found myself part of this
group without even having given my approval.

At that time, however, I felt that Sollers was
''sincerely'' siding with the leftist views. The fact
that this group put Foucault and myself in charge
of the Cérisy debate (No. 17) seemed to confirm my
feeling.   Another point in common was our interest
in problems of linguistics, even more so after I had
them opt (spring 1964) for the linguistics and poetics
of Roman Jakobson and the Russian formalists. As
a matter of fact, I think that the only true common
denominator between us was our complete adherence
to Mallarmé — something fundamental to my way of
thinking — as opposed to a certain Sartrian ''negli-
gence'' with respect to Mallarméan upheaval. But
the differences here were based on the fact that I
felt a kind of political affection for Sartre, while

they hated him . . . . My last contribution to *Tel Quel*
(No. 30): a series of texts on Joyce and *Finnegan's
Wake*, with a long study by Jean Paris.

During the spring of '67, *La Quinzaine littéraire*
published a paper which I entitled "L'Ecriture mani-
feste" (Manifest writing), meaning by this writing
outside of itself, rendering obvious the latent discourse of desire which appears in the very story,
like the narrative that had attracted the Huns toward
the Occident. Sollers' reply in the fall of '67 was the
redundant formula of "textual" writing – "textual
writing as *real* history" – a new name for the "expression focusing upon itself." For *Tel Quel*, at the
time of the invasion of Prague in August '68, "the
most important struggle of all is that of consolidating
the group and the magazine." (No. 47, p. 142)

After my resignation from the committee, the
periodical praised itself in December of '67 in an
article in the *Figaro littéraire*, claiming their ideology
to be that of the "closed group," renewing its faith
in what may be alluded to as the most backward
aspects of a falsely Mallarméan aesthetics, so popular
at the beginning of the century in Germany and
during the period between the two wars – in the style
of George-Kreis or the Junger-Kreis or the rightist
youth movements. You could see an increasingly
stiffening literary ideology. And this activity within
the framework of a zig-zagging political point of
view: flirts strictly Brezhnevian, at the time of the
invasion of Prague – this support of the invaders of
Czechoslovakia was necessary to "consolidate" the
group and the magazine, as they said – then, with a
comical shift, to a "Maoist" or "Chinese" point of
view.

The declarations of the so-called "movement of
June '71," a type of double of this group, were
ludicrous illustrations of what took place. In spring

'63, Tel Quel denounced in venimous fashion the
fact that the Movement of March 22, the ferment of
the May upheaval in its totality, was "suspicious"
(and called it "psycho-socialism!") But Marx had
said: history always shows its comical side after
the tragedy.   Four years later, under the name of
"June Movement," the group Tel Quel attempted to
become a burlesque copy of the great May-June '68
movements: to become also its own comedy.

In the summer of '68, when all extreme left
revolutionary movements born from the May riots,
and the French Communist party, strongly condemned
or disapproved of the invasion of Prague, it might
have been "fashionable" to adopt an opposite point
of view, just as it had been in 1960 when all the
authentic writers in France sided against the French
policy in Algeria.   When asked about the invasion
of Prague, Sollers answered (*Nouvel Observateur*,
novembre 1970) "our fight is elsewhere: it is on the
level of writing."   This "writing," which alone
"would weigh more than the liberation and the struggle of the workers' committees, students and writers
of an entire nation," can indeed be "textual:" this
is exactly what Artaud was talking about when he
asserted that *all writing is nothing but filth*.

A contemporary magazine defined such a group
perfectly when calling it a "neo-rhetorical school."

Let me give you some parrallel quotations, more
precise than any comments.

Tel Quel	*Change*
Declaration (No. I, spring, 1960)	*Havana Manifesto* (Jan. 8, '68)
Ideologists have ruled long enough over expression . . . it's about time a parting of the ways took place . . . let us be permitted to focus on it (expression) alone"	Writing is precisely this immense network . . . within which things of the world and gestures circulate: our work

consists in making this change visible.

Communiqué (Figaro littéraire)

"Tel Quel is a tightly closed group."

(Casas de las Americas, No. 50) Liminare (July 1968)

"Here is a revolution which is creating itself and is rewriting its science."
(*Change* I: *Le Montage*)

Epigraphe (No. I, 1960)

"I want the world and I want it *as it is*"-

Epigraphe (No. I: 1968)

"The activity of man which draws his own picture of the world, *changes* reality."
(id.)

Q.   What are the viewpoints expressed in your magazine *Change*?

A.   We try to *perceive* "change."

The movement "*Change*" was born from a poem. Written by me in the summer of '67 on an archipelago in the middle of the Atlantic Ocean.

It was also linked to the foreboding of the great upheaval that was unleashed in 1968.

At the end of October 1967 — on the 20th — I had my last meal with Sollers. We had just met Chklovsky, the last survivor of the Russian formalists, at Léon and Svetlana Robel's home. Sollers' strongly sarcastic remarks concerning Che's death and the revolutionary position of Régis Debray, which he considered "suspicious," were the last words I could stand coming from him. It was during the weeks following this meeting that the collective *Change* took form, among friends. The decision was made rather suddenly (by others than myself) to entitle it "Change" — the name of this poem written in the summer of '67.

What did this mean? The first statement we made concerning our viewpoint was made in Havana, in January of the great year '68 . "For the New Novel, literature was a static representation in a darkened room, a *camera oscura*" — and that is what the epigons of Tel Quel have been using like a caricature, that's what their title means as well as their initial Declaration No. I, which they never altered: "to want the world and reality as It Is (Tel Quel): rather than contesting it, representing it."

As for us, on the contrary — "it is a question of making visible, of taking apart the underlying mechanisms involved in representation" — but the truth of this tension resides in linguistic strength. The power of *change,* always present in our vision of the world is a mute linguistics. This does not mean that literature must become political economy. Its function consists in showing the power of change, via a network of language. The world in which we live is one of innumerable gateways; and each thing may be changed into something else by means of these very "gateways," *the function of change —* the function of language and writing. Our goal consists in making this change visible.

One of these "gateways," which are also sluice-gates — is called Berlin. The reason for all the transformations of the "Hexagramme" is to research it. But the year 1968 stirred this network — not only in the Latin Quarter in Paris, but in the entire world, from Berkeley to Warsaw to Milan — the network of struggles and the network of narratives. Societies everywhere began focusing on themselves, with renewed virulence — in order to *change.*

We live in *montage* societies.... No sooner
has a society suddenly fallen to pieces, revealing
its very joints, no sooner has it started to *verify*
its own trials, fusing the critics' struggle with a
criticism of struggle, than a revolution comes into
being.... (*Change*, I, July, 1968). Do you mind my
repeating what we wrote? If only to show you that,
contrarily to others, we do not reject what we have
said.... We do not play around with the idea of
replacing permanent revolution with a perpetual
palinode. Especially: we hate what an observer of
fascism called, before the second World War, the
"war of perpetual changes of front," the very es-
sence of the fascist phenomenon, particularly when
this war is skilfully introduced into the very heart
of worldwide leftism and consists mainly in con-
fronting "orthodox Brezhnevism" with "Maoist leftism." Then vice versa is the same way. The games
of literary men are unimportant in themselves. But,
among other things, they are symptomatic of something. To understand through these arbitrary meanderings the "literary economy," the *inside* of the
general economy of languages and struggles, *is*
revelatory. It is somewhat similar to writing under
the dictates of a dispersed unconscious, the flut-
terings and contradictions of the world body, of
human material. This *diaspora of the unconscious*
comes from the mouth and tongue of man just as it
emerges from his hand and sex organ. To say that
it permeates his "language" is to say that it courses
through the entire body and its power of *reporting
things* in all ways, in the dual sense of reporting
things: to bring, to report. *This* is what goes through
this archipelago which is the body, like a larger
hand opening upon colliding currents.

What constantly amazed me, from that time on,
was to see how this archipelago of the unconscious

and language materialized in its successive waves
of poetry and fiction, or theoretical criticism. That
of Jacques Roubaud and his brothers: Arnaud Daniel,
Dante, Hopkins. Of Jean Paris and his dangerous
friends: Leopold Bloom, H.C.M. or Panurge. From
Léon Robel and his companions at war who lived in
perpetual danger. theoreticisns of Central Asia and
adventurers: Eisenstein, Polivanov, Brik, Soulei-
menov, the Khazak. From Jean-Claude Montel and
Yves Buin, brothers of Artaud and Trakl; Philippe
Boyer, son of Breton and Bataille. That of Mitsou
Ronat, young sister and theoretically a student of
Noam Chomsky and Michel Leiris. That of Danielle
Collobert, younger sister of Sam Beckett. That of
Genevievè Clancy and Michel Bulteau, sister and
brother of Jean-Pierre Duprey. I found recently the
following in Duprey: "What I am no longer belongs
to me. See the change."

I am certain that in this archipelago everyone,
far from wanting to look alike, comes from *elsewhere*,
henceforth forming a corpus which does not look
like anything and travels alone within the very fiber
of the language which is common sharing to all —
"made by all, not by one." On its way, it breaks
those old crafty tables.

Q. What are your plans for the future in terms of the
novel, poetry, and as the editor of a magazine?

A. My plans: to draw a big diagonal ... The one going
through and through the *Hexagramme* of the six narratives, the six cities. The one around which it
bends. Or which pulls the *opposite* sides.

I am thinking of this obvious Chinese political
proverb: "the line is the main rope of the net; when
pulled, the links open."

As far as the position of the collective, *Change*,

is concerned, it is coming out regularly and with many ventures. Without ever rejecting what we have stood for, without lying to ourselves — we never stop moving.

PHILIPPE BOYER

INTERVIEWER'S NOTE:

Philippe Boyer was born in Paris in 1931. After studying at the Sorbonne from 1951 to 1954 under Gaston Bachelard, he worked at odd jobs, among them road-building. He then accepted a position which took him to Vietnam from 1961 to 1964. Back in France, he started writing literary criticism for *Esprit* and other journals. In May, 1968, he met Marguerite Duras, Nathalie Sarraute, and Jean-Pierre Faye, and became a member of the collective, *Change*. At this time, he also began attending the seminars of J. Lacan. He is the author of three works: *Watchwords (Mots d'ordre)*, 1970; *No Place (Non Lieu)*, and *The Split (L'Ecarté(e))*, 1973. To work for a living in order to remain free from the exigencies the public makes upon a writer; and to express his ideations as openly as he sees fit and in the manner that suits his temperament and taste — such are the elements of Philippe Boyer's oredo.

(Philippe Boyer's interview appears in the form of a letter).

Dear Bettina,

Because of the difficulties in answering your questions one by one, I joyfully accept your suggestion of a letter, in which I can freely pick up the different points you touch on. I leave to you the choice of what you will use of my varied reflections.

To start: there exists an almost insurmountable dif-ficulty for me to speak (or write) about my own writings. I believe (contrary to common belief) that the relation between the one who writes and the one who eventually speaks (or writes) about these writings is in no way an identical relation. It is, rather, a relation founded on the complex, highly diversified game we play, which radically *separates* one from another. So it is only in this *space*, this *gap* (which my third book, *The Split*, undoubtedly tried to fill), that I can try to say something about these books that hold a strange place in my life, as you can see. As I picked them up again in order to answer your questions, I realized that it was both impossible for me to read them, and impossible to recognize myself as having written them. (Which does not make it very easy to talk about them!) It is, therefore, from this no place (*non lieu*), if I may put it that way, where I am no longer the reader nor the writer, but the very *gap* between the two, that I will attempt to outline a few points at random.

This *gap* might serve as the entry into a reading of my first two novels, in the sense that they materialize the breach that the third book entered, in order to write itself. Thus, we can already locate between these two books the entry of an elemental bipolarity, analogous to the parental couple, as the first identification of the difference between the sexes. *Watchwords* actually settles some accounts in the domain of law and ''In the name of the Father;'' *No Place* proceeds rather toward transgression and incest, echoing the thought of J. P. Faye: ''Is not every (maternal) language clear, like every mother is pretty?'' That every mother is *beautiful*, no child doubts — and even, precisely, ''*l'échappée belle.*'' *(Certain key words lose their multiplicity of meaning in translation. Here, for example, although the phrase means ''to have a narrow escape,'' Mr. Boyer is playing on "l'échappée"* (space, interval, glimpse, escape, etc.) and *"belle"* (beautiful, and also a character's name in *No Place*). Of course, all this did not appear to me until afterwards. There is no premeditated intention on my part when it comes to disposing of the direction of what writes itself in each book, and from book to book. Perhaps this will become clearer if I am more precise about the strictly *material* way in which the book writes itself. There is, first of all, the title, which is announced from a distance like an approaching ship. Then comes the period of accumulating raw material — the incidents and events of daily life; from this accumulation, the outline of a possible narration is traced. Gradually, the writing unfolds, and it is possible that in the process the title must adapt and adjust itself to the mechanism of accumulation. This apparently risky way of production, without preliminary design — in no way deliberate but rather the act of a quasi-organic necessity in the sense that I would not know how to write otherwise — may have some connection with the way dreams are produced. "Book work" and "dream work" seem to have at least this much in common: both maintain themselves only by aiming at the realization of an unconscious desire. However, this difference (as well as others) must be kept in mind: if the dream operates by short-circuiting forbidden and censored things, the book, conversely, like all processes of sublimation, allows the realization of an unconscious desire only by subtly detouring the *"montages"* which constitute every process of change of form. But let us return to the first book, *Watchwords (Mots d'ordre)*. The title contains several possible meanings: the watchword that sets off an action; the written word of established order and of repression; linguistic and gramatical word order, which the writer strives to upset through his own style; the basic law of society, in which a word forbids — for example, incest. Here, it is a question of destroying the established order of language, of leveling

off the logical articulations of the signifier, upon which the unreasonable logic of desire is patterned. It's also a question of *"maux"* (A play on words: *maux* (evils) and *mots* (words) are homonyms) *d'ordre* as well, a narration of which is attempted. All this exists, to be translated in this book, to be transformed through what can be called an operation of "putting in fiction" — in the mathematical sense of putting a problem "in equation," that is to say, "in form." This operation will, of course, play on all registers without being truly controlled on any: register of the unconscious (fantasies in which the "woman in black" is a kind of messenger); register of the narrative (as the only possible support for what will unfold in this "book work"); and register of all social discourse (master/slave relation, relations of alienation) in which language, wherever spoken, is constantly penetrated. From another point of view we can also find in the narration itself the three instances of the real, the imaginary, and the symbolic — as defined by Lacan.

In this apparently innocent exercise in writing, we are dealing with the consequence — death — of completing a name, just as in the children's game of "Hangman," where a gallows is sketched and a man hanged, limb by limb, if a wrong guess is made. The desire is to write the forbidden name, which will result in the hanging of the man, and, therefore, death. To realize the forbidden desire — which in this case is also to return to the womb — is to die.

It would be gratuitous to say any more about these works, which require a mode of reading completely unrelated to the so-called "intentions" of a so-called "author." But all this tells nothing more than what is already *written*. There is undoubtedly nothing more to say. I believe that there can be no serious reading that does not demand of the reader that he expect from none other than himself the meaning that will sustain and realize his own desire to read.

I would nevertheless like to make one more remark
elicited by your questions. Certain critics (or even simply
friends) have often stressed the destructive, solvent,
negative character of my books, with their decomposed
reality, their shattered characters, etc. And then *No
Place* is obviously a title that clearly establishes at
the outset a deliberate negative intention. In reality,
perhaps, it is not all that simple.

The forbidden name, in *Watchwords*, leads us to the
story of the following book, *No Place (Non Lieu)*. The
title refers to the place of the book, which is invented,
fictitious and non-inhabitable. If the place must assume
a name *(non lieu* [*Another play on words: non lieu would
be translated "name place."*]), it would be Belle — image
of the Mother, whose body represents forbidden desire
and inaccessibility of love. And, finally, if writing is
the equivalent of killing reality (by rendering it fiction),
the crime can only be classified as a *non-lieu* in the
juridical sense (insufficient grounds for prosecution),
because there is neither a victim nor an assassin.

The surface of the page is cold and smooth as a
mirror, in which the untouchable heroine, Clarisse, sees
herself. On the page (the mirror) must be put into fiction
a realization of her forbidden desire for incest. To do so,
the mirror must be broken — by some act of violence corresponding to the crime (in this case a fire), which leaves
behind it charred ruins: the black and white that have
finally come to be written.

In any case, as far as I'm concerned, there is no
doubt that these two books wrote themselves in a totally
affirmative perspective. We would still have to agree on
what is being negated or affirmed. The least we can say
is that the death impulse has its word to offer here.
The fact that writing functions in many respects as a
petrification of reality is certain. But it is also primarily
a *"machine désirante"* ("desiring machine"), to use
Deleuze's term, and it is principally as such that it must

be made to function.

Regarding the narration (stories, landscapes, characters), it is perhaps through its "defects" that we can best understand the affirmation that it is in the "failures," the word games, the phonic associations, etc., that the "book work" is allowed to manifest its desiring functions, thereby driving the reader to the affirmation of his own desires.

Moreover, it seems to me that to introduce here a perspective of "negation," "decomposition," and "dissolution" does not work without making reference to the order (and evils) of ideology. Negation of what? In relation to what? To *make* the character shatter, one must first suppose that there exist somewhere "unshattered" characters, that there exists a unity, a totality of subject, all assembled under the unquestionable guarantee of a *name*.

You remind me that the name of Roussel was mentioned with respect to *No Place*. I don't think one should see here any kind of kinship, aside from fleeting surface effects. (Dare I confess, by the way, that Roussel bores me terribly?) The play on language in Roussel seems to me to result from a perfectly controlled, calculated, and predictable game. What I try to do (without ever getting there, ideally, of course) is to allow to come to the surface of the narrative as it writes itself, any and all associations that come under the pen. (This is generally indicated in the typography of either parentheses or, if it involves narrative discontinuity, dropping the type one line.) These associations naturally include not only thematic associations but anything that can be at play in language itself: displacement, assonance, gliding of one letter to another, permutation, etc.

Beyond what one might attempt to draw on the surface of the narrative = this narrative texture whose written *body* is so well veiled = I think (wrongly or rightly) that the book's true coherence lies solely in what escapes the control of the one whose motivation for writing is precisely to assert that control. This coherence is to be *read* in the zones of greatest freedom where, in a way, the book writes itself. These haphazard tracings (which are nevertheless perfectly determined by the logic of the signifiers that put unconscious desire in place) finally distribute on the surface of the narrative the real effects of sense.

My third book, *The Split (L'Ecarté(e))*, occupies that space between the first (*Watchwords*), which refers to the Father, and the second (*No Place*), which refers to the Mother, and embodies both genders, masculine and feminine. *(The title in French is rendered in both masculine and feminine forms.)* This third book, which lies between the parents, is the child, and is, therefore, the spreading of the legs in childbirth. The book, then, requires a change in language – a new language – the language of the child as opposed to the traditional language of the parents. There are "games of desire and the letter" that are to be related, as they play themselves in the first two books, and as they replay themselves in this third book at the same time that they are being related.

Now, to dwell on an aspect of your questions that I have somewhat neglected: it is quite evident that these books do not write themselves in transparent space, asepticized, impermeable to all external influence, to all those networks that weave themselves everywhere – networks of discourse, certainly, but also of events, social relations, economic circuits, etc. At the present time, I would say that one of our major preoccupations at *Change* is the questioning of the mode of production of any discourse, starting with underlying structures that articulate what we call, in the most general sense of the term, "grammar." It might be worthwhile at this point to go back to a discussion of the relations that established themselves among these three books, as they were being written, and the ensemble of discourse that has been developing during the last few years under the sign of

Change. Specifically, when I said that these books attempted to take into account, in the narrative itself, the ever hidden effects of this "underlying logic" of unconscious desire, I think such a perspective can find its place in the ensemble of the work of *Change.* This suggests, at least, that the narrative process stems from a mode of production that escapes the system of control. So, what is important — as much in the production of writing as in what we may call the production of reading — is that the "work" of this "*échappée*" be neither systematically repressed (as it is in all commerical literature) nor denied or prescribed (as it is in every literary endeavor with pseudo-scientific concerns).

In order to stay within this temporarily limited perspective of mine (literature considered as a practice involving the realization of an unconscious desire), which immediately recalls the personal history of the subject who is writing, one is obviously confronted with the fundamental question raised by Deleuze and Guittari in *The Anti-Oedipus:* the question of the ideological falttening of the oedipal triangle and the "family novel" and the way in which the story of the subject comes to be caught in the great social machinery. But I believe I am going a bit astray.

I return to your question about the influences that may have been at work in these books under discussion. I won't enumerate all my readings through the years, but I don't believe them to be any different from the ones that occupy all those who have been associated with literature over the past twenty years. But I shall mention two "meetings" that were probably very influential: with Bachelard, whose courses I took at the Sorbonne for three years; and, fifteen years later, with Lacan, whose seminars I have been taking for a few years. As for the rest, I am probably in a bad position to evaluate "influences" on me.

I will conclude, then, by answering your last question: "Where is the novel going?" This is a question to which I can offer no possible answer except to keep on writing. I would say that the novel goes where it can, but it certainly moves. Personally, I don't really believe in any "death of the novel." The novel will not be definitively exterminated by some mythic tidal wave of the comic strips or the so-called audio-visual media that guarantee that we'll all remain deaf and dumb. I believe that the good health of the novel has not ended. Whether we like it or not, we will have to keep on telling and writing stories.

Nor has the novel stopped *changing form*, of course. But is this not the dream of every writer — to write a book that resembles no other book? The novel is going — primarily, perhaps — where the reader leads it, reinventing at each reading, giving it its place in the ensemble of that polyphonic score of social discourse which has not ceased to concern us: we who are continually alive only if we are speaking and writing.

Translated by Cécile Insdorf

YVES BUIN

INTERVIEWER'S NOTE:

Yves Buin, a psychiatrist trained in the Freudian school, was born in 1939 in Paris. He was associated for quite a few years with the hospital at Ville-Evrard, in which Antonin Artaud had been interned, and now he is assistant at the large psychiatric hospital in Paris called The White House. He is very much engrossed in a new project: a therapeutic community which he is trying to found.

Connected with the Extreme Leftist movement from 1957 to 1965, Buin was more keenly interested in the revolutionary aspects of politics from 1965 to 1970. It was at this juncture that he discovered the 'counter-culture.' He is the author of five volumes of fiction, among them: *The Alephs (Les Alephs)* (1965), *The Vertical Night (La Nuit verticale)* (1970), *(110th Street, East)* (1972), etc., and he has written two theses: *Jean Reverzy* (1914-1959): *The Pulsion of death and writing*, (1968); and *The European Period of Wilhelm Reich*, (1972).

Buin has written extensively in newspapers and magazines on jazz, poetry, and on daily life. In 1966 he took a year's sabbatical leave to write a film scenario on America, "Pannonica or Insolent America." The project never came to fruition. Buin became a member of the collective, *Change*, in 1970.

Q. Why are you interested in the novel?

A. I am more interested in *fiction* per se than in the novel; fiction as it used to appear in the works of Edgar Allan Poe or in the simple narration of relationships in the *story*. Objects and themes can be almost unlimited in a story; they can vary from a play of colors to a description of a political rally. The novel, in its traditional sense, imposes a *coercive* form: characters, the story of their relationships, dialogues, etc. Narration or the creation of fiction allows for the mixture of different forms without accepting necessarily their conventions. In any event, I called my first book a novel because it seemed to me that I had always wanted — and I believe everyone dreams of such a goal — to write a novel. Later on, I felt freer and called my book a *story* even though the editor wrote "novel" on the cover.

Q. Were you influenced by certain novelists? painters? composers?

A. There were so many influences in my life that I sometimes ask myself who really influenced me. The list of writings which comes to mind is incongruous and strange: *Nadja* (André Breton), which is not a novel; *The Red Grass (L'Herbe roue)* by Boris Vian; *The Stranger* by Camus: *The Old Man and the Sea; The Monkey in Winter (Le Singe en hiver)* by Blondin; *A King without Entertainment (Un roi sans divertissement)* by Giono; *Desert of the Tartars (Désert des Tartares)* by Buzzati; a short story by Le Clézio, *The World is Alive (Le Monde est vivant)*; and *Naked Lunch* or the works of Dashiell Hammet.

This list indicates how varied and how commonplace my readings have been. Blondin, for instance, whom I know only through his books, is far from following the same path I follow. *The Monkey in*

Winter, which I have read and reread, is one of the most beautiful and tragic books I have ever come across. I also read Blondin's *Mister Long Ago (Monsieur Jadis)* and I believe the first ten pages are absolutely masterful. I would never be able to write like that. Yet, I do not feel any kind of envy toward Blondin. I must go elsewhere.

I will omit the names of the great classical writiers. Because of the difficulties I encountered in the French educational process during my elementary and secondary school days, I find it difficult to experience "French classical literature." That asphyxiating climate during my early school days compelled me to seek my contemporaries. Now it's very hard for me to go back to those men who have been buried under the dust of the university. I am certain, however, that I owe a great deal to those somehow neglected readings and probably much more than to the obvious names I quoted above.

Surrealist influence was of great import to me. I often reread surrealist writings, but more and more with pangs of nostalgia, as if I had nothing more to expect from that explosion that took place fifty years ago and which probably helped me to discover my own self. But one must do his own thing.

As for the rest—music and painting—I will be brief because it is from them that my most lasting discoveries have been born. I see the world as a fresco and I probably write the things I could never paint. As for music—and to me this means jazz—I have been totally imbued with it since 1945. I consider myself a jazz musician who writes. I often think that all I can claim to know totally is jazz and its history. My first published work in 1959 dealt with jazz and for ten years I have written a great deal on jazz and free jazz. I have probably written too much, since I now feel incapable of writing any

more about it. At this point I should like to speak
about Charlie Parker and about the important place
that his music has in my life. Maybe I am a little
presumptuous.   Do my writings speak of anything
else?   I never cease to be haunted by this music.
René Char once said that such encounters occur once
in a lifetime and that they are of extreme importance.

Q. What are the themes in your first novel, *The Alephs?*

A. I conceived that book almost ten years ago. I had
    had a strange dream, almost a nightmare: a man,
    long dead, came to bring me a message. During the
    night I wrote down the dream, and I engaged in a
    number of free associations, while fully awake. Then
    I sometimes recalled the lines I had written; but
    mostly, I thought about the rather bewitching presence
    of the man who appeared in the dream. I also became
    interested in the theory of numbers at that time and
    one day I read a chapter on *transfinite* numbers of
    Alephs. During the same year I visited two Mediter-
    ranean countries, Sardinia and Algeria: the first,
    just before the tourists' "colonization;" the second,
    just after the departure of the French colonists. A
    last aneceotal detail: I finished my medical studies
    at this point and I began to specialize in the field
    of psychiatry.   All of these factors — a dream, a
    multiplicity of rather sumptuous images (paintings?),
    a mysterious name, Aleph, and my first contact with
    insanity — must, without my being aware of it, have
    been instrumental in arousing my interest in writing.
    These various factors slumbered in me during
    my numerous nights on duty (one every four days)
    at the hospital.   Then I started to write.   It was a
    kind of apprenticeship for me.   I was proving to
    myself that I could make sentences; that I could let
    myself go. For the next three months I began telling
    myself stories. I created literature for myself, using

characters with whom I identified and who must have been alive in some way within me.

It is a love story (absolute love, as they said) which takes place in a world upset by a planetary catastrophe (atomic death has been suggested); the survivors, most of them young, return to the deserted cities, beaches, etc. and rediscover the splendor of the world. At that time, I was unaware of the newly-born 'counter-culture,' but I suppose I had many unconscious affinities with what was going on in California at this time. My themes were not very original: life, love, death — all set against a background of mathematical daydreaming and of sweet schizophrenic delirium (I may be exaggerating a bit). Furthermore, Aleph is the first letter of the Hebrew alphabet, which leads to the necessary and inevitable fascination with *origins*. We know that this quest is far from over!

Q. Is your concept of the novel similar to or different from the esthetic of Butor, Robbe-Grillet, Sollers, Sarraute, Ollier?

A. I choose Sarraute because of her intuition of those imperceptible variations and inner movements which have been called *tropisms*; Claude Ollier because of his notion with regard to fiction, writing which tries to go beyond the usual categorizing and labeling. I do not, however, consider myself part of the "esthetic community" which you mentioned.

I should like to add the name of Marguerite Duras: *The Afternoon of Mister Andermas (L'Après-midi de Monsieur Andermas)* (1962) and *The Ravishing of Lol V. Stein (Le Ravissement de Lol V. Stein)* (1966), both of which seem to me two remarkable works from a narrative point of view.

I am suspicious of the entire conceptual and

academic apparatus which has come to the fore in France today — Structuralism, Marxism, Psychoanalysis — often viewed narrowly, from an imperialistic, even terrorist point of view. It is the victory of scientific knowledge over *experience*. Actually, I believe that the writing of fiction is an experience. Fiction calls for the resources of the imagination. But it is by definition inseparable from the symbolic, since fiction is language. If I compare the two, I would say that narrative resembles more free association or dream (the royal way towards the unconscious), than rationalization, which, in its seductive coherence, represents, in fact, the major obstacle to any exploration of that same unconscious. I fail to see why a theory of writing should pre-exist the actual writing of the work or how it could influence a creator, except in an unfavorable way — which is the case of any repressive conventions adhered to in advance.

My psychoanalytical training accounts for my interest in the psychoanalysis of art or in the manifestations of insanity. I know — or rather I think I understand — that in the field of 'art,' and most specifically in literary works — we are confronted with perversions, incest, narcissism, compulsive repetition, etc. But how does such a situation influence a project which seems to emerge from me? I use a methodology formulated by others and apply it to my own work. For instance, my doctoral thesis was devoted to the psychocriticism of a relatively unknown French writer: Jean Reverzy. Although the method I chose may be questioned, I think I have shown in this work the relationship between death and writing. Reverzy died long ago and his work is, in fact, nothing but an object: five books left to explore and all literary devices were allowed: thematics, linguistics, syntactics. What would all of this have meant to Reverzy originally? I assume that from darkness (his own anguish, obsessions, his relationship with death) his writing was born to exorcise self-destruction. But Reverzy had to write this book for us to realize what compelled him to express his painful need and associations.

I myself am discouraged and probably afraid to project my own creations in an objective light, thus artificially disassociating myself from something which belongs to me and about which I cannot be indifferent. I would probably find myself in a primary narcissistic attitude — the contemplation of myself when in the acting of writing. I shall let Robbe-Grillet phrase the idea: "I write in order to find out why I write."

Q.   How do you create your works? Do you have a method? Does your unconscious play a role in your work?

A.   I have no method per se. I leave a **great** deal to improvisation as such. It may happen that a combination of words or a sentence imposes itself upon me. I then write it down. I often daydream while listening to music. Images — from an infra-verbal level rise to the surface. I try to capture them in their immanence. I know it is hopeless. I accumulate, therefore, heterogenous elements. It is the title, in a totalitarian manner, that organizes everything in my work and even explains it, leaving nothing to chance. From that point on, the nucleus of my writing is established. The overall picture will fall into place not in accordance with conscious logic, but rather following the dictates of imagination. This dynamic has not failed until now. I have reacted against it and sometimes very strongly, maybe because I feared too great a freedom of expression, or the danger of not being able to communicate.... I have very few illusions concerning the extent of my control over my work. To quote the theories of the *nouveau roman*: "it is the doing that does." The end result is never the initial design. Many writers share this opinion even if they express it in a more theoretical form. It is impossible to dissociate form and content. (Form/content, typical false problem).

Form imposes itself, and its contingency is only apparent: the form is the book. Even if he rejects a few of his books, a writer must realize that although some of them are already obsolete, even as he was writing them, imperfect as they are, they could not have been any different. You must not think, however, that I am in the process of yielding to an implacable determinism. No, things are more subtle and supple. We can always rewrite; one idea can transcend another.

Q. Can you tell us how *The Alephs*, *Round About Midnight*, *The Story of Smagg*, *The Vertical Night*, *110th Street*, *East* came into existence?

A. *The Story of Smagg*, which I wrote in 1967 at a time when we wrongly thought that there was an irremediable "historical void" in the Western Europe, is an expression of my then militant impotency, and most probably my will to be militant. But this negative attitude with regard to politically inspired literature — at best, Sartrean existentialism; at worst, "socialist realism" — would require a lengthy development. I cannot really go into this now.

For the past ten years I have been an extreme leftist — and militantly so. For a long time I was really not able to adhere to the different cultural positions that I should have logically defended. But when I started to write I could, in a way, prove to myself that I would never be able to adjust to the "given" and super-defined framework of *committed* literature. In *The Story of Smagg*, for instance, I carry on a dialogue with Paul Nizan who was a very important writer who died much too soon. In *The Vertical Night* the dialogue is carried on with the Austrian poet Georg Trakl, whose last night I tried to describe in a combination of words, images and commentaries. As for *Round About Midnight*, although the book was dedicated to the free jazzman Ornette Coleman, I think I probably owe it to Thelonius Monk. You may know the theme of his most famous work, composed about 1940, called "Round About Midnight." I was about fifteen when I first heard it, when Monk came to Paris, and I was truly shaken. I have always known that I would write about it, some day. But maybe I see this pattern only in retrospect, and *Round About Midnight* has an entirely different meaning for me. Probably. Anyway, I have always considered this book as a structured improvisation based on "Round About Midnight," and I retain a discreet preference for this book which, I might add, did not elicit any kind of overwhelming comment.

I wrote *110th Street, East* after I returned to France from a trip to the United States in 1970. I crossed your continent. The impact of this trip was enormous. Quite a common reaction for a European! After three attempts I finally succeeded in writing "my journey", which was certainly an inner one. The title enabled me to complete the narrative. And the title incidentally sounds much better in French than in English. Its rhythm is richer in French. I placed the encounters in my **novel** on 110th Street, East. I reconstructed a totally mythical street. When I returned to the United States in 1972, my book had been out for several months. I went to see

the street which is on the border between Harlem and
the Puerto-Rican neighborhood. I had never seen it
before. Now it was an ordinary street in the process
of being demolished. It certainly had nothing to do
with the street in my book. I probably would never
have written the book in the first place had I walked
down the street on my first trip to the United States.
But it was the dynamic quality of the words themselves in the title which was the decisive factor in
this work. My inner journey is still going on. Each
new book is a journey. Another time, another space.

    "Themes" are of no importance to me. I do not
renew any of them. But do other writers function
differently?

Q.   How would you define a character or a protagonist
in your novels? What is the function, if any, of a
character?

A.   If you mean by characters the prototypes of romantic
heroes such as those found in the works of Balzac,
Stendhal or Dostoyevski, I must confess I feel incapable of creating such beings.

    I must turn to a paradox. I was impressed by the
review that Jean-Paul Sartre wrote in *Situations I*,
and later in *Situations II*, of Albert Camus' *The
Stranger*, and by his remarks about the character.
He criticized the fact that some authors write thesis
novels, create protext-characters who become signs
and symbols used by the writer, in order to formulate
an ideological thought — precisely the author's own.
But has Sartre himself escaped that pitfall? He
noted particularly that it was deceptive "to put oneself in the skin of a character," to predict his emotions, to share his states of mind.

    I feel no desire to perform the task of a puppeteer.
Outside of my first book which was really a kind of

apprenticeship, I have removed myself, as best I can, from my characters. What strikes me is the inconsistency of my "characters," or rather let us call them *silhouettes*. I describe *objectively*, as André Breton said, about fifty years ago, at the time of his disdainful and justified attacks against "literature," or as theoreticians of the new novel say today — individuals who live situations, who wander through cities. Increasingly writers will use "I" and tell "the story." This particular *"I"* is not I, however, it is a way of imposing an omnipresent if not omniscient character, whose story is going to be told. We have, then, someone quite alive and present (in the true sense of the word) — at least, I hope so. I do not think there is any literary artifice in this case. The *"I"* is a delusion. You probably know the "equation" formulated by Lacan: "I think where I am not, I am where I do not think." You are unlimited and free to say everything when using the *"I"* as a mask, as nothingness. (I am not preaching the irresponsibility of discourse, however, when I want to say things that are not "literary;" I usually say them through action). The writer is implicit in the *"I,"* but he is elsewhere, too. Nothing, therefore, is invented in my books, everything has been reinvented. Nothing is autobiographical, but everything has happened to me.

There is one tendency of mine which does trouble me: the invention of exotic names. Just as the title of my books triggers off a story for me, so does a name establish the "character" and his individuality, without imposing on him a given life and story. Foreign names represent for a Frenchman centers of autonomous attraction, which organize the plot. When I read the names Sal Paradise or Charlie Parker, Bud Powell, Miles Davis or John Coltrane — they exist as such and do not need my help to describe

them.   But if these names have something foreign
or odd about them it's because of their dual genealogies. I also have a double genealogy. I am Slavic,
from Central Europe, on the one hand; and Celtic,
on the other hand. We know that genealogies, even
remote ones, weigh very heavily on the unconscious
strata and in the transmission of the most operative
myths. Every name which recalls an image evoked
by a narrative "I," links to it, via the sounds of
its phonemes, the underlying history of a culture.
It is not by chance that most of my "characters"
are named after ethnic minorities, especially Jewish
ones because in Europe, we cannot forget what we
witnessed in our childhood: the yellow star that
distinguished some of our comrades from ourselves.
Underneath it all lies the unfathomable problem of
our origins.

Womens' names in my first book were: Naima,
inspired by a theme from John Coltrane, the jazz
musician, and which means in Morocco "Come from
Paradise;" or still another one, Manteca, borrowed
from a piece by Dizzy Gillespie. But all this is in
the past.

Today, names impose themselves upon me like
rocks. They do not reveal their secret. They do
have the power to organize major meanings. The
starting point is often impossible to foresee. Last
August, I was writing short pieces "just for pleasure," somewhat in the style of the Gothic novel.
At one point, I saw a liquor bottle with the name of
the brand on it: Ruby Sandeman. It occurred to me
that the name sounded just right. Probably, I was
just waiting for this kind of situation to trigger something off. The fragments started to organize themselves. And Ruby Sandeman is present in two recent
texts I wrote: one for *Change*, the other for a collection of poetry to be published in paperback. He

is nothing else but his name. I do not think I embody
characters in the flesh, but, sometimes, I create
mirror protagonists such as Smagg, who was my
agonizing political character in 1966 -7.

Q. How do you react to the writings of Ricardou, Deleuze,
Derrida?

A. My interest in the works of Ricardou and Derrida
are remote. Derrida's difficult works attract me because they raise the question of anteriority and prev-
alence, the relationships of Mythos and Logos. But
I am more familiar with the writings of Deleuze, more
specifically those about perversion and schizophrenia.

In *Anti-Oedipus (Anti-Oedipe)*, I see the begin-
nings of a new period of thought with regard to
psycho-psychiatry. Felix Guittari's name as co-
author, should also be mentioned. Let us keep in
mind a few central ideas in the work:
— The criticism of the cult of the family; that is,
the question of the necessity and the perenniality
of the triangular family structure (and its various
substitutions) as the only way of constituting a
creative and productive human psyche.
— To include the totality of human desire and the
analysis of the entire notion of fixed repression in
the combination of nature / culture. The return to
Freudian sources, so to speak, or the desire for
pre-eminence over all topical or economic categories.
— The consequent assertion of the productive and
creative role of this particular modality of psychic
functioning (the schizophrenic psychosis), where,
according to Deleuze, the *"all powerful" desire*
prevails. (This idea is opposed to Freudian psychoanalysis, which sees in the schizo, the absence of
individualized desire). This creative urge of the

schizo, projecting en masse all of its sexual energy, turns it into a machine which longs for revolutionary polarity. The paranoic psychosis, on the other hand, because it is based on the invention of laws and the play of forces subject to taboos (incest) increases, caricatures the repressive foundation of the established family and culture. This kind of paranoic machine represents, then, fascist polarity.

These points which can be contested and discussed, do not remove us from the question of writing. These machines seek to encounter and to penetrate the structure of language.

The positions of the schizo and the paranoiac, to which we may add that of the pervert, may be retraced in terms of language, which is a repressive system (syntax, for example), an evolutive system (the containing words — James Joyce — or the dismembering of words — Artaud), and a subversive system (Joyce, Artaud, and Lewis Carroll, who, as we know, led the most perverse attack against language). In other words, every writer, as he faces language, can be submissive and accept the limiting apparatus which language represents: high-class language and its conventional appendages, its various styles used as a tool for discrimination. There we have the obsessive and paranoic use of form. Or else, the writer attacks the edifice, counteracts the traps set by convention, invents a quasi-schizophasia at the risk of incommunicability. One is tempted to draw a parallel here with the language of schizophrenics: Jean Paris, a member of the collective *Change*, and one of France's great Joyce specialists, has shown that despite the invention of lush and polymorphic words (*Finnegan's Wake* remains one of the most beautiful examples), the so-called schizo literary text actually respects syntax, versification, etc., just as music's freest types of improvisations respect form.

The subject of perversions is of utmost interest to me. We know that both the paranoiac and the perverted (the schizo is unaware of it) are defined in terms of the law. As Serge Leclaire (a French psychoanalyst and a student of Lacan) wrote: if the perverted and the paranoiac invent laws (so that the paranoiac conforms to them), the perverted does so in order to violate them. When a pervert writes, form is apparently respected. The reader will not find any attempt to break up the syntax nor vertiginous verbal proliferations. The text is readable. Yet, uneasiness and even anxiety result. The words are comprehensible, the rules are known, the structure is coherent, but the meaning escapes. The reader will live the deviation of meaning born from a series of inner meanderings within an apparently balanced text. I shall allow myself a rather obvious comparison. Let us say that both the pervert and the neurotic can perform similar acts: voyeurism, for instance. But the latter (the neurotic) will do it with anxiety, while the former (the pervert) will accomplish it with full satisfaction.

Perverted writers play with meanings rather than with words. *"Logic of Meaning"* by Deleuze suggests many views with regard to words, structure and the progressive loss of meaning in such texts — with regard to both the schizo and the perverted individual.

In my opinion it is in the actual 'perverse' writing procedure (and Borges comes to mind) that the greatest pleasure can be discerned. Psychoanalysts have labeled the act of writing an incestuous attempt. I must be very schematic here and, therefore, may be misunderstood or raise many questions. When the schizo writes it is as if he were writing on the constantly effaced body of the mother; he is at the same time engaged in a vain and "mad" — anguishing — search for total fulfillment. The perverted writer reintroduces the pleasure principle, whereas the schizo bases his literary attempts on fulfillment which, in our terminology, means the pleasure which would have been experienced in an incestuous act with the mother. The perverted individual differentiates very well between reality and fantasy. The perverted writer may know that the creative act is a total act (as is the joy experienced with the mother), but he has renounced it. He knows the law in order to bypass it more effectively. He knows language better to play with it. The game is a source of pleasure. A book does not exhaust him, and calls for another; just as an incestuous fantasy does not exhaust the real body. The symbol (the *location of meaning*) is situated midway between fantasy used as such and reality. The schizo, on the other hand, will try to confuse the real and the imaginary. The pervert will not confuse the two. He will use the symbol with perfect expertise and knows full well what he is doing. In the case of the paranoiac, writing will always be accomplished and experienced as part of the father's will, since the incestuous desire focuses on that image.

Q. How did you get involved in *Change*? What is your function in terms of the collective?

A. The facts are quite simple. For many years I was active in the students' political organization — the extreme left. I was active on the national level and organized political-cultural events. These did not go unnoticed during the years, 1960-65. I met many people at this time — many creative ones. For this reason I have never had any problem publishing my works. I concede, however, only in a minimal way to the publishing system: they publish my work.

In 1964 I was editor-in-chief of the newspaper, *Clarté*. Jean-Pierre Faye helped us fight bureau-cratic stifling. In 1967 I met Faye again at the National Vietnam Committee, and in May, 1968, we were both present at the founding of the "Writers' Union," which, as you perhaps know, was (for two months) a gathering place for an exchange of views among writers, students and printers. I ended my collaboration with that Union in 1969. It is not a coincidence that the collective, *Change*, approached me in 1970 and asked me to plan the issues entitled "Violence," conceived by Jean-Claude Montel. These issues have defined most clearly the political orientation of *Change*. And since that time, I have been included in the review. I have neither the linguistic nor the philosophical training, nor the reputation of the majority of the collective's members. My participation can, then, be understood in the following manner: my "politicalisation," my "spon-taneity," my association with outsiders and "de-viates," my deliberately non-academic point of view. I am trying to vitalize these views in *Change*. Our tasks are not stereotyped. We all have our certain areas and we respect each other's work within the collective. I consider myself the editor of works of fantasy, where imagination is called into play. But I am not the only one to possess this kind of quality. I call upon young poets, non-orthodox psychiatrists, etc. When I joined *Change* I said to myself: "I am here to publish the unpublishable."

Q.   Where is your novel heading?

A.   I would like to offer two examples of the type of literature that attracts me; and both are certainly well known to American readers. The first is *Bird* of *Paradise* by Laing; the second, *The Death of the Family* by Cooper. I am not discussing the psychiatric ideas implicit in these works. My only concern lies in finding a structure that allows *expression*. Both Laing and Cooper have attempted a kind of collage, of montage: the experience of relating an inner voyage with clarity, including in it the political dimension of daily life, the use of the metaphor, of the poetic "short-circuit," of assumed ideological empiricism, etc. We find in the premises and advent of the "counter-culture" many examples of the same kind of freedom applied to predominantly theoretical speeches. Personally, I find in it an outlet for my own inclination for the baroque and for collage, which I probably owe to my surrealist readings.

My own writing at the moment follows various paths. I have no precise technique to explain my way of saying: "a cat is a cat." The only thing I do know is that *110th Street, East* is the end of a periplus, the termination of a voyage. Right now, I lack the breadth to undertake a long work. I am trying a variety of things: an experimental text dedicated to John Coltrane, for the German radio, but without music, using only the musicality of the human voice (I think I have found the coltranian beast); some texts for *Change*, for *Temps Modernes*, for *10/18*. I am also enjoying my association with Ruby Sandeman. An editor from the extreme Left has repeatedly asked me to write an "Essay" on insanity for a new collection. The seriousness of such an undertaking frightens me. I might sound old fashioned, but I share Carl Roger's thought: it is more and more apparent to me that I have nothing to say that people already do not know. Especially at a time when madness is being inflated in the French publishing 'market.' What can I say about insanity? And since Ruby Sandeman is becoming more and more a part of me. I think I shall take him "over there" — a realm which is still unknown to me. In this way, perhaps, I might find the necessary climate to inaugurate a new technique — a type of collage emerging from what can be born only out of experience.

Translated by Tayitta Hadar

JEAN-CLAUDE MONTEL

INTERVIEWER'S NOTE:

Jean-Claude Montel was born on November 1, 1940, at Rèze-les-Nantes. He studied at the lycée in his home town, and received his baccalaureat. He pursued advanced studies for a time and was about to complete a License-ès-lettres when he decided to abandon his formal education. He is a member of the collective, *Change*, and the author of *The Beaches (Les Plages)*, *The Carnaval (Le Carnaval)*, and *Melencolia* (1973).

Q.   What was your background?

A.   I don't quite know what you mean by that question. I can only tell you that I found myself writing a book (in this case *The Beaches*) after two great set-backs. One of them was related to the university, where I rather rapidly became certain that I would learn nothing there that I wanted to know, and the other to journalism, in which I had taken refuge, where I learned even more rapidly that there was nothing much for me there either.

   I venture to add that these two "experiences" were separated by a stretch of a year and a half in the army, twelve months of which were spent in Algeria, a few months before and a few months after the settlement at Evian. So much for my "biography" of the sixties, and the circumstances which led me to undertake *The Beaches*, after numerous unsuccessful attempts.

Q. Can you tell us about the genesis of your first novel, *The Beaches*?

A. This was my first book and, as such, autobiographical to a great extent, above all in regard to the proletarian, or rather sub-proletarian scenes ans surroundings which are evoked in the first part. But this should be discussed in more detail.

In this book, as in *The Carnaval* and even more so in *Melencolia*, the notations or biographical elements are not there as such. There is neither documentation nor representation, nor is there reminiscence. All of these elements are there only as camouflage, not to recount what was — the life of this one or that one — but, on the contrary, to permit the story to develop from what could have happened.

The Beaches opens with the death of the supposed hero. The story tries to take up what death interrupts — not in the name of a so-called narrator, not even an anonymous one as is the fashion today — and to draw it out beyond this mute, dead hero (Pierre) into the story that this silence of resignation, solitude, and bewilderment hides. From that point on, my intention was to tell the story of classes sacrificed by history, of their anonymous heroes caught up in this inhuman waste, of the hidden face of spoliation and of exploitation, and of all that which renders the hero unable not only to lay claim to stature, but also to tell about it. This impossibility of expressing oneself puts into question the validity of the entire Western literary tradition (and not that alone), which the partisans of the "new novel" simply continue. This was what Artaud meant when he said of certain among them that they made "a complaisant parade of ruin," for the purpose of profiting from it.

Q. What have been the most important influences in your literary life: esthetic, pictorial, musical? Can you supply details?

A. It is very difficult for me to answer this question insofar as I am equally interested in architecture (see *The Carnaval*, in particular), music (jazz or contemporary music), and painting. However, it is undoubtedly to painting (Italian and Flemish) that I owe the most. It is due to its influence that this "acuteness of observation," which all writing pre-supposes, continually develops and gains in refine-ment.

It is impossible for me to enter into details here. I can only refer to *Melencolia*, which is also a journey through painting or, if you prefer, a pictorial narrative between the two poles of painting: Italian (Piero della Francesca — Uccello), and Flemish (Rembrandt-Elias-Bouts). The title *Melencolia* and Dürer's engraving came only as afterthoughts in order to assemble and immobilize all the themes set forth within the story, just as in the engraving itself the bric-a-brac seems to hang on the meditation of the angel or on his impotence. For it is there that the ambiguity of this engraving lies, not, as in the case of Holbein, on the level of the vanity of the arts and sciences (*The Ambassadors*), but in their mockery as they lie more or less strewn about at the feet of the androgynous angel; all these "implements" that present-day archaeology brings to light and displays in that great silence in which all thought is per-ceived as a form of labor.

Q. Does your concept of the novel differ from that of
    Sollers? of Robbe-Grillet? of Nathalie Sarraute? of
    Ollier?   Of what do these differences or similarities
    consist?

A. If, on the one hand, the "hero" is indeed one who
    cannot and does not know how to express himself,
    or one whose life is devoid of adventure and does
    not provide material for biographical narration; and
    if, on the other hand, the means of narration, the
    language, is in no way comparable to any naive or
    dogmatic science, or even less to the ungoverned
    application of language that we see at the present
    time, then you will understand very easily in what
    way I feel rather far removed both from the person-
    alized subjectivity (despite his objectal alibi) of a
    Robbe-Grillet, or from the structural and caricatural
    "materialism" of Philippe Sollers.
        Nevertheless, I would not fail to point out how
    decisive the reading of Nathalie Sarraute, Robbe-
    Grillet and Claude Simon was for me in the sixties.
    They broke open many syntactical "locks" and
    cleaned up the French language by restoring its
    original precision.   And, rather curiously, it is to
    the syntax and language of the Middle Ages, in truth
    to the early Middle Ages, this language of generation
    and transformation, that they provided access.

Q. Is your novel committed in the Sartrian sense of the
    word? Is it politically committed?

A. I do not see how any writing, whether prose or poetry,
    could not be committed. This is why the concept of
    the *roman engagé* seems to me a simple tautology.
    But, since you refer to Sartre, and since that com-
    mitment in his case is apparently political, I will
    simply refer you to *The Paths of Freedom* (unfinished),
    which is undoubtedly the most summary and the most

false example of realism that we possess in our contemporary literature. Sartre's idealism and populism go back to the years which preceded the October Revolution. I am, at least with regard to this province of his thought, in theoretical and practical disagreement with him.

Q. What are your writing methods? Do you set up a plan? Does the dream world play a role in your work? Do you establish guidelines?

A. It is precisely because I never set up a plan that the sequences fall into place themselves (or do not fall into place, in which case they disappear), and the narrative proceeds from the writing itself. For writing a book is not engaging in politics, any more than in mathematics or in linguistics. It is rather the exact opposite. What is told and described is neither true nor false, nor the redoubling of truth, but the interweaving of the true and the false, the interlacing of opposites. It is their uniting, as much on the individual level as on that of society, in this dialectic between the internal and the external by which history "is made." In the case of Marx, as well as of Freud, it exists not on the level of their mythical complementary natures reduced to some Freudian-Marxism, but rather in their difference. It can also be criticism of the history that is "being made," the parallel narrative, whether secondary or hidden, which goes along with the other, attacking it or complementing it; the criticism of society precisely in the sense in which Marx uses this term as subtitle of *Das Kapital.*

Q. Can you explain to us the visions as well as the scheme of *Melencolia*?

A. What takes place here – the actions which are de-

veloped – cannot be taken over by characters. Indeed,
it is not a question of an individual destiny, but of
the whole in which each one, without knowing it,
has a role to play and plays it.

It is rather a question of quasi-characters, or
even more precisely of quasi-pronouns, of demon-
stratives in the grammatical sense of the word,
which are taken here absolutely. That is to say,
they do not represent any word, any adjective, any
idea, any clause; they have a nominal, undefined
function. They are also implements of syntactical
inflexion which can be exchanged for each other and
take over the discourse in turn, without speaking
(and even less acting) in their own name. They
permit the expression of a certain point of view in
the absence of the other nouns. In this way, what
one might call that "objective monologue" is progressively formed. For, in this enormous mass of
internal and external events, which increase and
which pile up one upon the other finally to constitute
"written reason" which is written and spoken daily –
nothing happens. In this place, in the heart of the
city where all social classes mix, this *young man*
stirs about on the fringes of all of them or at their
intersection. This young man from no class or,
even more precisely, *déclassé*, lives in a place where
the classes are oblivious to themselves, prey to the
magic lure of ideologies.

That is why these quasi-pronouns change names,
or rather, in the absence of other nouns, borrow from
them their linguistic functions, mimic, imitate or
pillage without shame for the sole benefit of the
narrative which, little by little, is made up of all
these contradictions and proceeds without a break,
even though – and above all – because it is *made up*
of all these breaks. These people are nobody and
say so, at the very moment when the opposite of
what they believe takes place and is achieved before

their eyes, removed from all language. They do the opposite of what they say and say the opposite of what they do. For everything seems to elude them irretrievably, including that control of language by which "the true criticism of society, society itself," is presented to the reader at its nerve center, where the hidden story progresses and offers itself as an absurd theater for marionettes, where the actors are only marionettes animated by their words alone, having no bodies but only corporeal attributes. But this mockery is not only a simple "lighting effect." It plays a serious role and, one might say, even a tragic role here. For the principle adopted is that of montage using documentation, but in such a way that the latter becomes neither stage, nor source of reference, nor foreign body, but disappears entirely in and of itself, dissolves until it is no longer anything but this modulation, which is unceasingly taken up again and again (and often in a contradictory manner), and by means of which ideologies "find their language" and never cease to unfold their story. That is why these quasi-characters, who think they are speaking in their own name, speak about someone else, always someone else. That is why what is told here is not a story, but that which makes all stories possible. The goal is neither a search for identity nor some quest for being through the example of individual destinies, but the effort to achieve "the range of a real method of operation" in this mass of events.

We have definitively moved away from the bour-geois novel, called novel of education (even though it is social here), for if these quasi-characters stam-mer incessantly in uncertain and vague places, or recite ridiculous odes to liberty in the manner of sleepwalkers, it is not because the story has ended for them but, on the contrary, because they are not yet part of it. They vegetate in words, speaking of others. And while they fade before your eyes, while their waiting and their silences tell of their own impotence, an apparently unequal struggle takes shape and develops progressively in the most secret part of the writing between *this one* and *that one,* who have been constituted with enough force and independence from each other to enable one to envisage the real terms and conditions of a confrontation.

Consequently, the endeavor described here precludes my even contemplating a description of the existence of these quasi-characters ("one thousand meter radius, no more, that is the circle of their existence"). I cannot depict them as happier than they are ("for it is in their room that they are miserable") and even less come to terms with their misery. It is merely a question of laying the foundation for a "full, transparent, and complete narrative," or, in other words, to compete with history, just where it seems to be least present, and on its own grounds.

Q.   Do you try to decompose reality or to reduce it to the level of nothingness? to dissolve the concrete image, to decompose or to disperse the personality of your protagonists, if they are indeed protagonists?

A.   It is easy to understand that for such a narrative nothing can be set aside, *a priori,* either on the level of dreams or on that of reality and its notations. The whole problem is to know how they will be reused, how they will gain new meaning. And this is done by the montage of language and its disassembling (Eisenstein), and by critical analyses of ideologies in the light of which individuals and societies, at a certain moment of their history and of their evolution, perceive themselves and tell about themselves. There, in the "lie" of history which is also its fiction, both prose and poetry take on the form of "memoirs," by the search for truth which gives birth to them, and by the language of *desire* which underlies them and which they transcribe in all of its exigencies. This is the prime requirement of man, confronted with his desire which always escapes him, and which seems always to move further away from him as he seeks it. This, the first fiction of man and of society, is the driving power of all narration.

Q.   You are part of the collective, *Change*. What are your functions?

A.   I do not have any "functions," strictly speaking, but, I hope I have a role to play through the texts I bring to it; that is to say, by a certain means of insertion in collective projects which are developed there, from one issue to the next.

Q.   What do you think of the ideas set forth by Jacques Derrida in, for example, *Grammatology or Margins or Positions?*

A.   I have no opinion about it for the simple reason that I have not read it and that I have not found any reason to do so up to now.

Translated by Lucille Becker

MARC SAPORTA

INTERVIEWER'S NOTE:

Marc Saporta is the author of many volumes on law, foreign policy, literary criticism, and American literature, and he writes experimental novels as well. Though friendly with Robbe-Grillet, Ollier, and other *"new wave"* novelists, Saporta refused to follow their metaphysical and stylistic credo. He branched out on his own, considering himself a renegade and a pariah. In this interview, he discusses at great length his novels, *The Ferret* (1959), *The Search* and *The Casting* (1961), *Composition No. 1* (1962), *The Guests* (1964), *May 1968*, and *The Girl on the Sidewalk Opposite*. Themes, objects viewed as people and people as objects, time-space concepts, the visual and the sensual within the framework of the narrative, tenses, punctuation, mobiles, games — all are explicated in terms of Mr. Saporta's own innovations.

Q.   What is your background? Can you give us some bio-
     graphical details?

A.   At the age of twelve or thirteen, I had already decided
     to write. I used to put down my jottings in little
     notebooks. What I wrote was abominable — really bad.
     Then, when I went to the university, I wanted to
     take my degree in letters. I started to, but my parents

preferred that I major in science. The compromise
we reached was that I should register for letters,
science, and law too. This way, I had a complete
range of possibilities. I dropped the sciences quickly (I really have no gift for them), and finished law
and letters. At the age of twenty-five, I found myself
with a doctorate in law, working as Research Assistant for UNESCO. For five years I worked in the
division that was formulating the world convention
on authors' rights; and since my vocation was writing,
I wrote some legal articles. By the time I was
thirty, I had to my credit an enormous juridical output, as though I were an old professor of seventy
years of age. I wrote juridical studies at the same
pace as others write novels. Then the convention
was signed, and I was bid adieu. In one way, it
was lucky for me, because otherwise I might have
published nothing but legal articles during my entire
lifetime, if I had stayed at UNESCO. It was at this
time that one of my very dear friends, Françoise
Giroud, told me there was a job for me with a new
scholarly magazine, founded under the auspices of
the U.S. government, to disseminate American culture
in France. So I began to write on subjects other
than law and after a few years, I had published about
fifty articles on American civilization, American
research, etc. Then came my first novel. My law
studies influenced me a great deal — for better and
for worse — in the same way, as it were, as my readings of Proust. They taught me how to "split hairs
in four," as we say in France. Law is a science in
which everything depends on the position of a comma
and, for Proust, life depends on the word one is
going to utter and the gesture one is going to make.
Therefore, it is necessary that just the right word
and not any other be used; that Mr. X and not Mrs. Y
present you to the Duke of Guermantes, and so on.
Law teaches you these things: to place the comma

and the word, not to mention the gesture, and even the object. Unhappily, a certain dryness results.

Q.   In your novel, *The Ferret*, do the objects determine the action?

A.   More than that.   The objects *are the characters*. This has provoked a misunderstanding between Robbe-Grillet and me.   When I took *The Ferret* to the Minuit publishing house, Robbe-Grillet was in charge.   He had already published his *Les Gommes* and *Le Voyeur* and was writing *La Jalousie*.   With *Les Gommes*, he had made his mark; after *Le Voyeur*, everyone considered him a great young writer.
     So I showed him my manuscript of *The Ferret*. I am one of those people who willingly recognize the influences they have undergone and admit to them fully; so I will honestly say that Robbe-Grillet, that day, even while refusing my manuscript, gave me some very interesting ideas which I put, or think I have put, into practice.   So I went back to him a few months later, after having reworked the text in accordance, I thought, with his suggestions.   Catastrophe! He said to me: "That's not right at all! You didn't understand a thing I said!"   I had interpreted the suggestions or ideas that Robbe-Grillet had formulated for me as a function of what *I* wanted to write. They had proved to be very useful, for *The Ferret* would not be what it is had our conversation not taken place.   But, obviously, Robbe-Grillet wanted me to write à la Robbe-Grillet, whereas I had used his very intelligent ideas to write à la Saporta.   He wasn't satisfied. He told me he would show the novel to J. Lindon, the director of Minuit publishers, to see what he thought of it.   Two weeks later, I received an insulting letter from J. Lindon (a man I respect greatly, for I respect my enemies when they deserve it): "You have parodied Robbe-Grillet, you

have used his techniques, but with a metaphysical
and literary view opposed to his.'' According to
Lindon, I had attempted to ridicule Robbe-Grillet,
which was not at all the case. I had simply carried
out my own research. At the time, we were all—
Robbe-Grillet, Ollier, Butor and others — heading in
the same direction; it was natural that there should
be some cross-checking and that we should reach
rather similar conclusions. In the end, we agreed
on arbitration with Robbe-Grillet, who was gentle-
manly enough to send my novel to Seuil publishers,
where it was immediately accepted. The result of
which was that, at Minuit publishers, certain very
stubborn people were long convinced that Seuil had
taken the novel in order to counterpoise against
Minuit an anti-Robbe-Grillet.

Q.   Will you talk about objects?

A.   This long digression is precisely about objects, because in Robbe-Grillet's work there is no anthro-
pomorphic dimension. Objects are absolute, neuter.
They are inert. What Robbe-Grillet reproached me
for was, precisely, for having taken the obverse of
his metaphysical view and for having made characters out of the objects; the objects cause the
story to advance; they were the novel. I had created
a world of objects. Writers never know right away
what they are writing: much later on, I said to myself that without realizing what I was doing, I had
put myself in a prophetic perspective, because
several years later everyone was repeating that we
are a world of objects and gadgets, and that objects
have taken charge of the world. Perec has even
written a novel on this theme: *The Things (Les
Choses)*. Many people began to vilify this gadget
universe, this consumer society. (I was not among
them, however.) After the fact, people always say

that writers know before others what is going to happen. That was true with me, with *The Ferret*, as it was with J. D. Salinger's *Catcher in the Rye*, for example. If we had known how to read Salinger in 1952, we would have known that Berkeley was going to explode in 1964.

In sum, in *The Ferret*, a man passes from one object to another; he circulates that way, somewhat under cover. Now, it's very curious to see how a minor incident, without any particular interest on the literary level, can condition a reflex over a long period of an author's life. In an article of no great importance written by Françoise Giroud in 1946, I think, there was mention of an imaginary family, one of whose sons had been a supporter of de Gaulle in 1941, and who had been executed; another, faithful to Pétain in 1944, had been executed, and so on; each had stuck to his view at the wrong time. In the family next door, there were also four or five sons who had been Pétainists, Gaullists, etc. But the Pétainist was a Pétainist in 1941, the Gaullist a Gaullist in 1945, so now they are all wealthy and highly considered. The implicit conclusion of the article was that many people choose the wrong *moment* rather than the wrong *cause*.

Before *The Ferret*, I had thought a long time about Françoise Giroud's article. I had understood the interchangeability of circumstances. The same object, seen at two different times and placed in two different places, takes on a different connotation and value. Certain objects, in certain circumstances, linked in a certain context, take on a particular coloration. A hatpin, with its little black head, can evoke in the mind of the character the tenderness of the moment in which he undoes the hair of the young woman when he makes love to her for the first time; but this same pin, described as a dagger in another chapter, in other circumstances and at another time, evokes cruelty and suffering. If I have succeeded in making that felt with my two descriptions of the same object, fifty pages apart, first after a love scene, then after a break-up scene, the reader will have understood what has happened in between, according to context; but the object remains the same. That's the meaning of the world of the object in *The Ferret*.

Q. Do eyes play the same role in *The Ferret* as they do in Robbe-Grillet's *La Jalousie?*

A. Certainly not. When I used Robbe-Grillet's ideas, I acted in good faith, inasmuch as I don't understand them at all. In his work, it is obvious that eyes are playing a specific role. Mauriac stressed that when he called his school "*L'Ecole du regard*" (The School of the Look). But the role of *le regard* in my novels is very different. I am tactile — completely concerned with touch. I have the impression that all the objects I describe in my works serve as intermediaries, as transitions; they have a reality quite different from their reality in Robbe-Grillet's work, in which they are only seen. *Le regard* is almost a subterfuge for me.

Q. Does man depend on the object in *The Ferret?* Does the object live?

A. I can't answer the second part of your question. We don't know what life is, so it would be bold to say that the object lives. We have defined biological life; an object, in this sense, does not, of course, live. But we can say that it has life in a certain sense. The perception that we have of it evolves, as though the object itself had evolved or lived. There is one thing that the Robbe-Grillet/Ollier group has reproached me for, and that is for having accorded a sort of will to my objects. Do the objects

have a will in *The Ferret* or does the invisible character bestow a will on them? It's rather the second
hypothesis. But I haven't settled the argument. I
have written what I could. One doesn't write what
one wishes; one writes what one can. As for the
first part of your question, the character depends on
the object. That is evident, and it is, in part, the
subject of the novel.

Q.   Why does the narrator commit suicide? What symbolic value has the rope as an object?

A.   He could not do otherwise. The characters impose
themselves on the author. One day I walked out of
Professor Fort's course at the Sorbonne because he
had stated that if Shakespeare had wanted to end
his plays differently, he could have done so. I got
up and walked out, slamming the door behind me.
If I hadn't already had my *licence* and my doctorate,
it would have been an act of courage on my part; but
I was simply taking a second *licence*, which wasn't
necessary for my career. I never went back to the
Sorbonne until this year, twenty years after, when I
was asked to teach a course there on the American
novel. The ideas I presented to my students were
diametrically opposed to those of Professor Fort.
    We can never really know how poeple write.
Most of them never tell us; they always find a good
way, *ex post facto*, to explain what they've done,
but we don't really understand whether writers lead
their character or are led by them. I firmly believe
they are led by the characters. If they want to
force the pace or jostle the character, the novel
stops. The writer has no more thrust, no more inspiration. He drops everything. My character commits
suicide because that's the only thing he can do, and
I can't do anything about it. Even though the woman
he was in love with is a bitch — she has two or three

lovers at the same time and she deceives him — still, when she leaves him, for him it's as though an earthquake had occurred. Now, this young woman gave herself to him perhaps capriciously, without really loving him. (We don't really know; we don't see her; we don't know what she's thinking.) And, in fact, no one is responsible if an earthquake razes your house. Love is an "act of God;" no one is responsible for the damage caused by the cataclysm. That doesn't prevent us, however, from despairing.

Q. In *The Search* (1961), the protagonists are two collectivities in confrontation. Can you tell us why the object as such has disappeared?

A. I must first talk about *The Casting* before I speak about *The Search*. The former is the link between *The Ferret* and *The Search*. It is the contrary of *The Ferret*. I had written a first novel in which objects were the characters. I wanted to experience writing a novel in which the characters would be treated like objects. I had described twenty objects in *The Ferret;* in *The Casting*, I described in the same way seventeen characters in a fictitious play. I placed them there, one next to the other. My decision for *The Casting* was never to tell the story. I was going to present the characters, and the reader had to understand what happened to them in the light of their description only. Moreover, I presented these characters treated as objects in the future. The object was there, but projected toward the future. It was the first time this had been done. There had been novels in the past ("he did this," "he was doing that"), in the present ("he is doing this or that"), but never in the future ("he will do," "he will do," "he will say"). Now, in *The Casting*, the play that is the subject of the novel is still unwritten; from the beginning to the end, it is a novel written in the future — a still shaky future, because it was a pioneer work.   Simone Balazar has done better in a book that appeared two years after mine and which took much of its inspiration from mine: *Next Summer* (published by Julliard).

Meanwhile, I had written *The Search* as a truly metaphysical experience.   It is probably the only novel that I am completely satisfied with, that is finished, complete — except that I have never succeeded in writing the last chapter!   I was overcome with fatigue.   I had composed the work in twenty nights and was exhausted.   So I made up my mind to end the work at the next to the last chapter (which is not necessarily the last one written, since I do not write chapters in any specific order).   In a way, I spent not twenty nights but twenty years writing it.   As a matter of fact, twenty years earlier I had read the dialogue of a seventeenth-century play *El Condenado por Desconfiado* by Tirso de Molina. It's about a holy man who has various experiences; who starts out in sanctity but, as he lives his adventures, ends up doubting his faith.   In the end, he dies in such a state of doubt that he condemns himself.   It's really the orthodoxy of the Spanish Counter-Reformation in its narrowest, most bigoted form.   But this bigotry reveals a curious broadmindedness as well, concerning redemption, because it applies dogma literally.   In this play, there is a brigand, a thief, a murderer, who at the last moment has a vision and dies believing; this is his salvation. (This is a scenic illustration of the theses of the Council of Trent.)   The schema of this work had very much impressed me, with its two movements, one ascending, the other descending, in the shape of a multiplication sign.   I used the schema for *The Search*.   Two opposing communities; two trajectories. At the beginning of the novel, you have this soldier, serial number 666 (a few critics have pointed out

that he bears the number of the Beast in the Apoc-
alypse). He is a beast. Material for the army. Almost accidentally, he kills a girl during a demon-
stration, without even knowing what he is doing but
with all kinds of sexual connotations. The gun
pointed toward the girl is the sex organ. He wants
to grab hold of the girl but can't. He is stuck in the
ranks with his gun; she is among the demonstrators
on the other side; he cannot touch her. But we say
in France "touch" in connection with the firing of
a bullet, too. So he has "touched" her anyway – in a
play on words but also a play on symbols: the jet of
the bullet as it comes out of the gun will "touch"
the girl, not to impregnate her, of course, but to kill
her. Impregnation and death are, however, in a
certain sense one and the same. The concept contains a whole symbolism of beast, sex, girl, rape . . . .

After he has accomplished the act, unconscious-
ly, like a beast, like a military animal, the soldier
starts his search, which continues through the entire
novel; he searches for the girl; he wants to know
whether he has killed or wounded her; as his search
progresses, he rises; he becomes conscious of what
he has done; he feels he is in love with this girl
who is dead or wounded – who is gone, in any case.
When, at the very end of the book, he is about to
make love to a prostitute who resembles the girl,
it is not purely coincidental that she is Spanish
(reminiscent of the play) and that her name is Alma
(soul, in Spanish): the Beast receives a soul. By
following this path which goes upward, in a certain
sense, through love, the soldier will rise. On the
other hand, the girl's brother (representative of the
opposing community), who is among the demonstrators, is an idealist. He is demonstrating for a
noble and generous cause. At least, he thinks he is;
young people always think they are fighting for
noble causes. I too have demonstrated frequently

for causes I believe to be noble. One of the reasons
for *The Search* is that at the time of writing there
were a lot of demonstrations in France, and I had
spent a night in jail for having demonstrated. Now
the soldier in question goes in search of the wounded
or dead girl, while the other fellow, her brother, is
in search of the one who shot her. He is moved by
the same noble spirit as when he went out to demon-
strate. These soldiers, he thinks, are our brothers;
these soldiers don't know what they are doing; I'm
searching out with a sense of fraternity the one who
shot my sister. I want to know who he is, explain
things to him, make him understand.

   And as the search progresses, it becomes a
hunt. He is the hunter; the other one is the game;
and he will be haunted not so much by the idea of
finding his lost brother as of finding his sister's
murderer. He takes the descending path, in his plan
for vengeance. The two paths cross, but the two
men don't know it: on the last page of the book, they
see each other but neither knows who the other is.
The soldier wonders whether the young man on the
sidewalk isn't the person who has been searching for
him so assiduously; the young man knows that among
the soldiers that are filing by is the one he has been
looking for. But it's too late. The regiment files
past. They won't see each other again. They have
seen each other without seeing each other. That's
the story of *The Search*. It's more complicated than
you think; it's a philosophical, metaphysical path.

Q. Why do you refer to your characters according to
   their physical traits or characteristics?

A. I am tactile and sensual; I have been reproached
   for not knowing how to describe men and for giving
   importance to women only – to woman's physique.
   This is true, in a way. There are objects and women.
   Men interest me less.

Q. Will you talk about *Composition No. 1?* What was your purpose in writing it? Why didn't you number the pages?

A. It's the same old problem. I had begun in the future with *The Casting*; I had written an essentially metaphysical novel with *The Search*. In *Composition*, there are at least three intervening factors. I'll tell you what influenced me: the greatest influence was Calder's mobiles, which I admire tremendously. Calder had conceived sculptures whose elements could move in relationship to one another. I wondered for a long time how I might do the same in the novel. Then I received from a friend two or three books (one by Steinbeck) in a French boxed edition. The books had not been bound because it was a de luxe edition, and for highly de luxe editions, on Japan paper, for example, it is customary not to cut the pages. The pages are not sewn together nor assembled in any way. They are printed, folded, and sold in a box. You are even asked not to read them, because to do so you would have to cut the pages. They are intended as booklover copies and collectors' items. For me, it was an inspiration to have received these collectors' items with printed pages that couldn't be cut. I thought to myself: that's how to write a novel like a Calder mobile. I shall write unnumbered pages, which I shall put into a box; it won't be a de luxe edition, since that isn't my purpose, but technically the material process would be the same.

Let's go back to Françoise Giroud. She had said that according to the time when things happen, events take on a different meaning. Contrarily, there was **Sartre's** old theory, according to which we are the sum of our circumstances, or our phenomena, of all that we have "existed," if you'll allow the expression, which is not grammatically correct. (Ortega

y Gasset once said: "I am me and my circumstances.") Now, in accordance with Françoise
Giroud's article that kept going through my head, I
kept saying to myself that if we add the same events
in a different order, the sum is not the same. I had
to find for my mobile novel a way of making that
explicit. And that's what I did, because when you
take the novel and shuffle the cards, i.e. the pages,
and you read in a certain sequence, the main character might turn out to be a thief whose talents are
used by the Resistance against the Gestapo; but
if the shuffled pages are read in a different sequence,
he might turn out to be a former member of the Resistance who was unable to get reinstated after the
war (as happened to several members of the Resistance who had been used for murders and thefts, and
who subsequently were unable to return to their
normal way of life). On the sentimental level, according to the sequence in which the pages are read,
it might turn out that the hero, during his adolescence,
had raped a young German girl in his parents' employ;
that he had subsequently sought a mistress who
resembled this young girl; and then, after having
been abandoned by her, that he had made a very bad
marriage. But if the pages are read in another order,
it would be about a young man who had made a very
bad marriage, who had raped a young girl in his
employ before taking a mistress who would avenge
the young girl. All combinations are possible,
according to the order in which things happen; and
the main character can be very unlikable or likable,
his adventure can be excusable or execrable, according to the page seuqence. So there is an anti-
Sartrian intention added to the Calder influence, and
all of this is expressed almost solely through ob-
jectified descriptions.

Q. What are the influences of Proust, Melville, Dostoyevsky and Faulkner, enumerated in *The Guests?*

A. If it hadn't been for Joyce, I would not have written
    these three monologues without periods and commas.
    Proust taught me how to split hairs. Dostoyevsky
    is the one who invented "the game" (*le jeu*) in the
    novel. A kind of game of truth. The game serves
    the purpose of moving the action forward, and in
    many of my novels there is a game. I have invented
    a game that didn't previously exist, and since it
    didn't exist, I was unable to describe it: the game
    of the wild hats, which I talk about in *The Guests.*
    (I wasn't even able to find out myself what the game
    was all about.) *The Casting* is a game too, of course.
    A social game: the presentation of a play.

    As for Melville, it's not just a coincidence that
    the French rediscovered him in 1939-1940 and that
    Sartre published *Nausea* at the same time, and that
    Nathalie Sarraute began writing. I have explained
    this in my *History of the American Novel* (Seghers,
    1970). Existentialism interrupted the natural course
    of French literature, or at least diverted it into a
    combative literature. Literature finally resumed its
    natural course with the "new novel" in 1955. Com-
    pare the rope in *The Ferret* with Melville's, and you'll
    see.

    As for Faulkner, he was one of the greatest men
    I have ever met. After his death, I went to explore
    that little town of ten thousand inhabitants — Oxford,
    Mississippi — where he had succeeded in reconstruct-
    ing the whole world from nothing. It is he who taught
    me, among other things, the value of great literary
    myths, and in *The Guests* there is a great Faulk-
    nerian myth with characters, however, who are my
    own, and besides which the book is made up of
    seriatim personal experiences. (There are even too
    many of them in *The Guests*: experiences with time,
    objects; calligrams taken, or almost taken, from

Apollinaire; words hidden in words, like in Cummings, etc.) The great myth in *The Guests* is the myth of God and the Devil. One of the characters, Luke, is the leader of the game, the master of the house; it is he who receives the guests and is in charge of the gathering. He has always been the one in charge of the gathering or the group; he is the mastermind, the creator. He represents my luminous side. I have projected into Luke everything I should have liked to be; whatever good is in me has been sublimated into Luke. Now Luke is going to die, and he knows it. His intimate friend in the group is Doctor Ty, who represents my dark side. He is everything I regret being. The two are my inner God and the Devil. If, one day, God should get fed up and give the world back to the Devil, and if the Devil should want to prevent the world from going straight, the poor Devil would be obliged to take good care of the world since henceforth it would be his. He would not be able to try to destroy it; but then another Devil would rise up beside him, and willy nilly, everything would start all over again, except that the Devil will now have assumed God's role, at his expense. To this, we must add certain considerations on the subject of death. This is certainly a very disorganized book, which I had been trying to write for a good ten years; and when I had finished writing it, I found that I had said everything. With *The Guests*, I ended one phase of my life and my work. Everything I had wanted to put into my novels over a long period of time, I had put into *The Guests*. I thought, I knew, I feared that I wouldn't have the strength to continue. In *The Guests*, there are at least ten novels that I have not written and will not write, but which I would have liked to write. Each time the characters tell about their life or I write their biography, it is a novel I would have liked to

write, and instead of writing them subsequently,
after *The Guests*, I stuck everything into *The Guests*,
and for that reason the book was considered a failure
by many people at the time.

Q.   You haven't written any novels since?

A.   Well, yes.   I have written two extremely important
experimental novels — at least I consider them extremely important.   The first contains only two words,
written on a paving-stone.   In May 1968, I took a
paving-stone from the street and painted on it *May 68*,
novel by Marc Saporta.   This novel tells the reader
a story if he experienced the "revolution" of May
1968, which we all experienced differently.   The
German BN had asked me for something to exhibit,
and I sent them this paving-stone.   It was a great
success.   I changed this object into a novel by virtue
of writing, the verb, the word.   You add a word to a
paving-stone and it becomes a novel, provided you
consider it as such.   It tells a story.
        I worked for a very long time too on another idea,
which a colleague stole from me in the meantime.
I had always thought that if you cut out all the articles
in all the newspapers on a given day, and if you put
them in a box, you would have a novel.   I talked
about this a little too much.   One of my colleagues
seized the idea on the wing, and wrote a novel about
an imaginary actress named AA (as Brigitte Bardot is
called BB).   He had cut out of some women's journals
and movie magazines all kinds of articles about different actresses; but he didn't put them in a box to
mix them up; he chose some of them and had printed
in sequence various articles that had been written
about different actresses.   By arranging them in a
certain order and by replacing each time the name of
the actress by AA, a coherent story resulted.   It
wasn't very well written, though, and wasn't too

great a success.

I have also written *The Girl on the Sidewalk Opposite*: a collective experience. I had proposed to nine of my colleagues a character (the girl), a place (the sidewalk), and a distance (opposite). Each one was to write in twenty pages a short story on the theme that I had proposed, and it was all to be published together, in a book to be entitled *The Girl on the Sidewalk Opposite*. The first reaction of the authors of whom I had made my request was refusal, on the grounds that you couldn't just place an order for their writing. Then, a day or two later, I began receiving their telephone calls, letters, and even telegrams, accepting. It was a nice experience and it's a great collection. Subsequently, two or three publishers have used the idea, revolving around other themes.

Q.   How do you manipulate the reader in your book?

A.   I don't manipulate him. I rely on his subconscious. I try to arouse it. All writers must reckon, involuntarily, with their readers' subconscious. I do it deliberately. The more clearly a story is told, the less the reader's subconscious can make associations. The less the story is filled in, the more the reader's subconscious will be able to construct his story. I give him as much freedom as possible; I provide some clues and some indications, but he makes his own association of ideas.

Q.   Have you written any plays?

A.   In 1967 I wrote for French Radio-Television a very long play in three acts, which was broadcast over three week's time, for one hour a week: *1917, Relief*, to commemorate the fiftieth anniversary of the entry of the United States into the war in 1917. I didn't write a single line of this play. I just cut up some 1917 texts and put them together, just as I did for the novel I spoke to you about. I have also written an unproduced play, *Komrade Elektra*, and a one-acter entitled *Moon Games*, which is a divertissement that has been produced only twice at festivals.

Q.   What are your future plans?

A.   I have a contract from French Radio-Television for something in the style of *Composition No. 1*. The same cues are proposed in two different sequences; the same dialogue is presented twice, changing the place of the cues... And this play, *Vice and Verse*, was actually broadcast on April 9th, 1973. And then, I still have a lot more books in mind...

Translated by Alba Amoia

CALUDE OLLIER

Claude Ollier was born in 1922 in Paris. A graduate of law school, he has been employed in business, industry and in the field of administration. Ollier established his literary credo in *The Setting (La Mise en scène)* (1958), which won the Medici Prize. In this novel, which takes place in a mountainous region in North Africa, Ollier attempts to create an atmosphere in which the author becomes non-existent; where descriptive details of gestures, discourses, events, souvenirs, though narrated in a most precise manner, leave the reader disoriented. The abolition of chronological time and conventional spatial concepts (by the opposition between facts as related by the protagonists and those with which they are faced) serves further to increase the contradictory, troubling and mysterious elements which the reader must sort out for himself. The action of *Law and Order (Le Maintien de l'ordre)* (1961) also takes place in North Africa and concerns a man who is to be killed by two armed men sent to follow him. Ollier's detached descriptions of the man's room, the elevator, the car ride, etc., heighten the anonymity of the protagonists, placing the burden of recognition and recomposition almost wholly upon the reader. In *Nolan's Failure (L'Echec de Nolan* (1967), the disappearance of a plane over the North Sea leads to an investigation by a mysterious "Agency,' thereby fostering a growing under-current of mystery and fright. In *Indian Summer (Eté indien)* (1963) and *Navettes (Shuttles)* (1967), characters are introduced as "absences," their identity and vitality depending almost entirely upon the depth of the void they create in the narrative. *Life on Epsilon (La Vie sur Epsilon)* (1972) tells the story of four astronauts who land on the planet Epsilon, the breaking down of their electrical equipment, and their subsequent loss of contact with the earth. Ollier's superb verbal translations of sensations, reminiscences, vibrations, color tones and para-rhythmics lend an outerwordly atmosphere to this fascinating work.

Q.   Can you tell us a little about your life?

A.   Yes.   I was born in Paris on December 17, 1922.   I studied law and commerce, then held various jobs in trade, industry, and administration, before eventually deciding, in 1955, to devote myself exclusively to writing.

Q.   Why did you choose the novel rather than the theatre as a means of expression?

A.   Theatre has never interested me very much.   Cinema, yes; cinema contains theatre, as well as other things, within itself.   In any case, both theatre and cinema are far removed from literature, which I have always felt to be my main concern — and music, but I've never gone into music.

Q.   What is the genesis of your first work?

A.   My early works date back to 1946-1947.   They are short stories, some of which appeared in the first part of *Shuttles (Navettes)* in 1967.   My first work of amplitude — if I may use that word — is *The Setting*

(La Mise en scène). It grew out of long years of contemplation of an outline map pinned on the wall of a bedroom, in the mountains, shaded from the African sun by palm trees.

Q. They say that, long before Robbe-Grillet, you were creator of the aesthetic of "total objectivity" in the realm of the novel. Is this true?

A. Robbe-Grillet and I, since 1943, have spent a good deal of time exchanging books, seeing films, and searching for a definition of literature. We used to compose short texts simultaneously. He is the first one to have undertaken a work of "amplitude," and he created a new pattern in novel narration.

Q. Just what is meant by "total objectivity?"

A. I don't think I have ever spoken of "total objectivity." But perhaps my memory fails me.... If I have spoken at times of "objectivity," it is due to inexperience or analytical error. I do not see language as subjective or objective. You might say that a piece of writing is "objective" when it seems to describe objects beyond awareness or áttention, and "subjective" when it seems to be more or less closely connected with such awareness or attention. In any case, everyone talks about objectivity, but what does it mean? As far as I'm concerned, nothing. The distinction [between objective and subjective] perhaps is meaningful if you think literature is supposed to concern itself above all with psychology or with "revealing" the mentality of an author or his characters, or the like. But you can say that *Jealousy (La Jalousie)* is a totally objective as well as a totally subjective novel; and the same goes for *The Setting.*   Therefore, the distinction is not at all

relevant.   There are grammatical forms that refer
back to a noun or pronoun subject, and others that
refer back to a noun or pronoun object — that's all one
can say.   Literature is a selection and combination
of grammatical forms, and not an appendage to psychology.

Q.   What is the necessity of such objectivity or dis-
simulation on the part of the author vis-à-vis his
creation?

A.   The author does not create.   As Valéry said: "The
author is positively no one."   The person who writes
invents new combinations on the basis of old ones,
and any one can do that — provided he is a good
reader.   Literature is not primarily a question of
expression (personal, social, political...).   It can
be that, but the result is a distortion of the world
through the critical use of its languages.   To know
whether the "author" brings himself forth in his
"work" or dissimulates himself is a falsely posed
problem and a terrible misunderstanding, which you
can play on, of course, by assuming the form of this
confusion in order to demystify it.

Q.   How do you compare your visual technique to, for
example, pictorial art?

A.   My technique is not visual at all.   Moreover, I am
a mediocre observer. If my books sometimes have
"pictorial" or "cinematographic" aspect, it is
because the reader, in spite of himself, likens the
effects of his reading to those of the reading of a
painting or a film, but it's not my doing at all.

Q.   In your novel, *The Setting*, you create a scene exterior to the characters and events, which really
functions as a stage backdrop. The human being thus

becomes fragmented, disparate, despite the fact that he is described in minutest detail. In order to understand him and to grasp the role he plays in your work, he must be reconstituted by the reader. Why do you find this complicity between the reader and the author so important?

A.   It's not a question of complicity, but rather of joint effort: the writer sketches the hollowed out meaning of the book, and the reader fills in the hollow. They say this began around 1880, with Mallarmé, but I would go back at least to Flaubert and Poe. *Madame Bovary* provided significant directional signals; it's up to the reader to heed them. A book is a piece of research, above all; the researcher has no idea where he is going, especially at the start. So, one imagines a narrative support, commonly called a "character," and a prop for this support, called "world" or "décor," and one conceives a relationship between them analogous to the relationship that seems to exist between writer and language. Later, one perceives that the reader of the text finds himself, vis-à-vis the text, in an equally analogous relationship. The wandering search is shared, and the reader becomes basically part of the text. As for man's "fragmentation," that is a certainty, and the act of writing does a great deal to intensify it.

Q.   Is *Law and Order (Le Maintien de l'ordre)* a detective story in part? Why are the new novelists attracted (if indeed they are) by the detective story?

A.   I did not try intentionally to make *Law and Order* a detective story, even in part. You could say the same about all of my books. It just happens that, by my particular use of existent narrative formulae, in a demystifying perspective, I end up using them now and then to make my point. You might even say that

Indian Summer (Eté indien) is a musical comedy;
I often thought as much as I was writing it. Literature thrives on imitation, and the succession of
different texts through different epochs constitutes
a long chain in which each link is more or less derived
from the preceding ones. In this way, Borges and
Benveniste are linked up. The relationship between
the text and the "author" is completely secondary:
he is anecdotic, and never explains anything.

Q.   How do you create the haunting atmosphere of your
     novels?

A.   I'd love to write a gay, carefree, serene book. Maybe
     I'll succeed one day. But the basic relationship
     between man and the world is a relationship of
     terror – born of the juxtaposition of two worlds. All
     important films are horror films (Murnau, Bresson,
     Eisenstein, Bergman); all important books, too (*Don
     Quixote, Bouvard and Pecuchet, The Future Eve,
     Locus Solus, The Adventures of Arthur Gordon
     Pim*...). If the atmosphere in my books is haunting,
     that's fine. I would like it to be terrifying. After
     which, I'll write a happy book.

Q.   What do your characters – who are comparable to
     essences or rather absences stalking through your
     work – symbolize?

A.   There are no other symbols in my works than those
     internal ones necessary for the construction and the
     coherence of the fiction. My "characters" symbolize
     absolutely nothing. They exert themselves in re-
     flecting on the world which surrounds them, that is,
     the fictional world – which is to say, literature. If
     anything "stalks" through these works, it is un-
     doubtedly the feeling of uselessness in their exer-
     tion.

Q. How do you create? What is your technique? For example, do you outline before writing? What is your procedure?

A. In the beginning, each book is like a global, nebulous image. Writing the book is really making a rough sketch of this image while extracting its virtualities; geometric forms emerge from the image, and then take on more figurative contours. The writing of the book is the struggle between the text as it writes itself and these initial shapes. The book composes itself step by step, word after word, and it is given to be read word by word. The story that unfolds is the meaning of fiction. My "procedure" consists in choosing and combining the words most likely to resound and to constitute the autonomous being composed of internal dependences — which is fiction.

Q. Which authors have influenced you most? Which painters? Which musicians?

A. The authors that have influenced me most are Jules Verne, Poe, Flaubert, Villiers de l'Isle-Adam, Raymond Roussel, Borges, and Shakespeare. As for painters, Kandinsky and Bosch; musicians, Debussy and Schonberg; film producers, Lang and Bunuel. I'd like to say a word about jazz, about Parker and Monk: I paid a small but heartfelt token of homage to the latter in *Indian Summer*.

Q. And Jules Verne?

A. Jules Verne is the only author I had read up to the age of eighteen. He was living literature as opposed to the dead teaching of literature that I received in school. Jules Verne undoubtedly saved me, in this sense, from complete disgust with literature, which I felt when listening to the functionaries whose duty it was to teach love of literature. I hope things have changed since. (I'm talking about the days before the Second World War.) In any case, it's Jules Verne who showed me the pleasure of discovering something through narrative, through the very exercise of writing. Others, of course, later filled this same function: Flaubert, Poe, Dostoyevsky, and Raymond Roussel, who worshiped Jules Verne. Jules Verne stresses the mechanics of facts, the finite of a plot, and relegates to the museums the horrors of psychological analysis of the humanist novel. It is in homage to Jules Verne, to Lévy-Strauss, and to Henri Michaux that I have written in these past years my three "science-fiction" books. I wanted to put into narrative rhetoric the very idea of science-fiction, and Jules Verne's enthusiasm, in the course of this difficult task, has been a constant source of encouragement.

Q.   Would you analyze one of your novels — *Nolan's Failure (L'Echec de Nolan)* for example — from the point of view of themes, artistic vision, characters, symbols, etc.?

A.   *Nolan's Failure* is principally a rereading — therefore, a criticism — of my three preceding works. The "themes," therefore, are those of the three books, plus the theme of their reading. But I don't know what an "artistic vision" means. Their is nothing beyond a linguistic point of view, that's all. The "character," in this case, is the reader-writer. "Symbols," here too, are purely internal in the universe of fiction; they refer to nothing external. Each reader obviously is free to read as much as he wants in the wrong way. Certainly, the effects of "representation" are inevitable — in the prolongation of our idealistic ideology. But that is just what has

to be eliminated, and *Nolan's Failure* "says" just
that.

Q. Wherein lies the mystery of your novels?

A. Mystery lies in the origin of language and its pro-
liferation.   What interests me is the relationship
between man and the world of language.   Psychological analysis is unimportant for me.   If I thought
that the human being should remain ambiguous, incomprehensible — as certain people say — I would not
write.

Q. Why always mysteries, investigations?

A. The dialectic analysis of events implies a detailed
and circumstantial description of them.   Since most
facts seem extremely mysterious, there is nothing
surprising in that long, detailed investigations are
required to penetrate their obscurity. But this answer,
in the critical perspective of the Sorbonne, is only
an abrupt reply.   The investigation is the one con-
ducted in the wild, bushy land of narrative forms in
order to dislodge the idealist ideology.   Mysteries
are those posed along the way by a tradition of
obscurantist reading.

Q. Would you talk about violence, as well as mystery,
as presented in *The Setting*.

A. If there is violence in *The Setting*, it isn't spectacular; there is a filigree of violence throughout,
undoubtedly, but it is veiled and diverted.   For example, the successive movements in a murder are
decomposed and described separately, in several
scenes.   This may be due to a personal aversion for
describing violent acts, but certainly more to the
idea that the more a description is allusive, the

more impressive it is. It's the same in the movies: displays of crude horror strike you at the moment only, whereas suggestions of horror remain alive in your mind for a long time. Moreover, for *The Setting*, the construction of the plot required that the story that had already taken place — the violence — be evoked only very skimpily, in disjointed bits, just as the newly arrived engineer came to know about it, either directly or by hearsay. So it was in the very planning of the book that the violence that had occurred a few weeks earlier in the mountain should become manifest only as traces, as graduated signs along the path. Thus, the violence is simultaneously on the path, in a composite or traces, and in the head of the one who finds the traces.

Q.   What do you mean by reality, especially with respect to the engineer in *The Setting*?

A.   The reality of a book is the totality of its text. But "daily" reality is made up also of texts of an accumulation of texts. Things in the world never reach us directly; they always pass through stages which are the languages used to give them form. The reality of the world reaches us only in the form of commentaries, and these commentaries are always impregnated with the ideological coloring proper to the place where they originated, whether it be in economic, philosophical, political, or scientific discourse. In *The Setting*, the reality of the mountainous terrain which the engineer is exploring (by the reality "inferred" from the text is meant the reality of the ensemble of indications furnished, not the reality of the "referring" terrain which you can amuse yourself by trying to identify for the text and which perhaps provided certain materials); this inferred reality, then, slowly takes shape for the engineer out of the commentaries provided by the interpreter (his guide).

For, in this story, the languages used in the country play less a role of stages than of obstacles, since the engineer does not understand them. What does the engineer find? Some signs. But these signs have no value for him, inasmuch as no commented discourse explains their origin, their nature, their destination – that is, their MEANING. So it's actually a trick commentary that the engineer hears – precisely the commentary corresponding to "the setting" that the interpreter creates in order to hide from the stranger the true unfolding of past events. Why this setting? Because the events that take place in the tribe are not the business of strangers, generally speaking, and here, more specifically, of colonizers. The latter have conquered most of the country, but have not really settled except in the fertile regions (the "useful" country, according to the colonials). Thus, the regions in the high mountains are left more or less free of the colonizers' deeds and ges- tures, and remain the responsibility of an auto- chtonous administration. The colonials live on the edge of the plain, close to their small forts which are equipped for emergencies. But they nevertheless control from afar developments up on the mountain, and important matters must be brought to their at- tention – murders, for example. Thus, the engineer is doubly suspect in the eyes of the tribe: first because he has come to make a land survey of a mining trail which, if acquired by the company that has hired him, will mean for the heretofore tranquil village the arrival on masse of trucks and white technicians; secondly, because, arriving on the scene shortly after the drama of his predecessor, he will not fail to uncover the traces of the murders and get himself involved in them. So it is urgent to "take command" in order to find out, first of all, what he has decided about the mining trail, and, secondly, how to get rid of all the traces, or at least how to lessen their import. So it is not an exaggeration to say that this "setting" is a collective reaction of the members of the tribe, and the old soldier who gives the orders is the agent working for the protection of the tribe. The old soldier, Ba Iken, is simultaneously the guide and the interpreter. He is the "dragoman." (Interpreter, in Arabic, is "torjman.") Through him, the engineer learns the realities of the tribe. He knows the two languages spoken by them — Arabic and a Montagnard dialect — and he knows French. He speaks French using a syntax which combines in a strange way Arabic and French syntaxes; his vocabulary, too, combines elements of the two languages. The principal axis of the book, then, is the axis of the dialogues between the engineer and Ba Iken, that is, the one according to which the "valuation" is made between true and false among the bits of information furnished and commented upon by the interpreter. Indeed, everyone "interprets" the facts in this adventure: first the engineer, whose unexpected task it is to do so; then Ba Iken, who does everything possible to guide his judgment; and little Ichou, who offers himself as an assistant and tries to establish a setting contrary to Ba Iken's in order to thwart his plans. (Ichou is the one who wants to emigrate, who will leave the tribe and make his way in the "West.") The engineer's interpretation turns out to be right; he foils Ba Iken, slowly, but with a sort of irregular tenacity that one would scarcely expect of him; he proves to Ba Iken that he has contradicted himself, but doesn't push his advantage too far because, in the meantime, he has gotten to know the country in all its aspects, and he is captivated by it. What he finally will discover — the reality of the two murders and the identity of the guilty man — he will keep to himself in the end, and when he goes back down into the plain, he will not breathe a word of his discovery in the mountain. A tacit complicity between him and Ba Iken will cause him to subscribe to the setting organized in his honor: he will be loath to stir up quarrels, whereby he would play the role of spy or informer, certainly; but also he will respect tribal "consensus" and understand the Montagnards' point of view. After all, it was just too bad for his predecessor; either he didn't realize what he was doing or else he knowingly and rudely violated the law of those whose guest he was. In both cases, he was guilty. But the engineer's feelings are nonetheless more complex: he would have liked, in a way, to live his predecessor's experience in his own turn.

Q. How do the threats and signs increase in *The Setting*?

A. Threats and signs in *The Setting* are laid out in the circular itinerary followed by the protagonist. As one leaves the plain, two roads are open to anyone who wants to go up the mountain to the region of Imlil (in Berber: white, the center of the white zone on the map): the road on the right, along which the adventure will unfold harmlessly, and the road on the left, where it will end tragically. Generally, travellers go up one road and come down the other, thus making a complete circle. Going up on the right, the engineer whom we are following in this adventure finds traces of the course taken by his immediate predecessor — an unfinished course, inasmuch as he was killed half way up. Signs of his presence are strewn along the circular course, and the engineer (Lassalle) comes upon them in reverse order — not only in time but in space. He lives his own experience forward, we might say, and he simultaneously lives his predecessor's experience backwards. The circular trips are joined at the beginning of the book — in Chapter 3, specifically — when the last link of the chain of the past "hooks up with" the

chain of the present: the glance of the dying girl
in the white room of the infirmary catches the engineer's glance and the instant of that glance is like
a fast-motion film of the tragedy she has just gone
through.   It is this glance which alerts Lassalle,
in many ways: first, because it arouses the suspicion
that something abnormal has happened here a little
while ago; next, because he feels that they are
"expecting" something from him, but he is not too
sure of this; finally, because he is possessed by a
troubling feeling that if the girl's glance was so
sharp at the moment of her death, it was because
she had just "seen someone again," and all throughout his own adventure, Lassalle will act somewhat
like a ghost.   Thus, the threat unfolds along this
circle, and for a long time Lassalle believes it is
directed against him.   He spends most of his time
making the distinction between the signs pertaining
to him personally, and the signs pertaining to this
sort of "double" who ventured out here before him.
And then, one fine morning, he becomes convinced
that all the threatening signs concerned the double,
that he had done nothing more than review them
mentally, in their reflection already paled by re-
moteness and by the dawning of oblivion. From that
point on, the book hastens toward the fastening of
the circular itinerary.   All has been said.   The
threatening signs have been removed.   The last
chapter unfolds in the same place as the first.   The
scorpion, dreaded sign of terror, has been eaten by
the ants.

Q.   Does the reader find out why a man is awaiting death
     in a North African city in *Law and Order*?

A.   The reason is given very early in the book: the man,
     who has discovered the criminal actions of some
     racist policemen and who is suspected by them of

wanting to denounce them to the higher authorities, is the victim of an intimidation whose purpose is clear: if he talks, he will be killed. This is the anecdotal reason on the detective and political level of the book. But the real reason stands out against a backdrop of waiting which is much vaster, according to the terms imagined for the construction of the book — that is, the alternation between exterior and interior. Standing in front of the wide bay window of his apartment, facing the white city in which he works, the administrator-hero of the story finds himself permanently in an uncomfortable position, dissatisfied with both sides of the "barricade" raised by his window against the world. The blinding summer light that comes from the ocean shore and unfurls over the city invades his room and lays the foundation for the oscillation, the vertigo that divides the sections of the books into its lancinating counterparts. Here, too, the "reality" of the city reaches the ears of the protagonist only after having been filtered through the commentaries of the autochtones: the conquerors know nothing, or prefer not to know. Blindness, in every sense of the word, is the central theme of *Law and Order*: the blindness of the colonizers, the blindness of the police who exercise their privileges in a blundering manner, the blindness of the witness of their plots, on the seventh floor, who wavers, hesitates, is bewildered, in three hours of reflection on three busy days, in a too subtle use of tenses. It is by the appropriate use of temporal syntax that the steps of the hero are marked, almost continuously "impersonal" in the grammatical sense of the word, but which a pronoun, here and there briefly personalizes, as though inadvertently. What he is waiting for, really, is the end of the author's hesitation between maintaining certain classic narrative forms, typical of the traditional psychological detective story, and the search for new forms, more

appropriate to the creation of the textual environment
from which his adventures derive. What is he waiting
for, finally, is the death of that author.

Q.   What is your opinion of the novel today in France
      as well as in America?

A.   The novel today, in France, is emerging. After the
      "New Novel," there was "Tel Quel" and Jean-
      Pierre Faye, Ricardou, and Maurice Roche. Now
      there is Guyotat. Unfortunately, I am not very familiar
      with present-day American novels. On the other
      hand, I know the films better, and in this domain
      many things seem fascinating to me. Purely com-
      mercial novels are selling well in every household.
      The type of novel that concerns us will continue,
      no doubt, to fare badly — that is, will reach an ex-
      tremely limited public.

Q.   Will you tell us about your radio plays?

A.   I have written seven radio plays. Some are tra-
      ditional dramatic compositions (I had to "get used
      to" this kind of writing — I had no idea what writing
      for the radio was like); others are based on sonorous
      narrative research. Several are the development of
      pre-existent literary texts. Thus, *Regression* is the
      development, with recitative, numerous dialoguing
      voices, and musical and sound effects, of a short
      text published in the collection *Shuttles (Navettes)*:
      The Ranger's House (La Maison du garde). These
      works for the radio, as well as two or three works
      which I wrote for the films, constitute to my mind
      the general system of my books, and should cast a
      new light on some of my works. They are like little
      satellites retransmitting the most recent information
      about these texts. As for the system of my books,
      it is a spiraloid structure: the first spiral contains

the first four books, *Nolan's Failure* taking up again
the material of the first three and fastening the
circle; a second spiral also contains four books,
three of which have been written thus far: *Life on
Epsilon (La Vie sur Epsilon)*, *Enigma*, and *Ur or
Twenty Years Later (Our ou Vingt ans apres)*. All
the books are connected by several networks of
analogy or of opposition. The global fiction that
emanates from them can be read in fragments, book
by book, in no special order, or can be read in its
historic development, in succession, and this way,
perhaps, all the corresponding networks appear.

Q.   What are your future plans?

A.   I'm writing books and a radio play. Television
interests me. I should like to take a trip around the
world by ship and read *A Thousand and One Nights*
in the original.

Translated by Alba Amoia

JACQUES BOREL

Jacques Borel was born in Paris on December 17, 1925.
His father died shortly before his birth. He spent his
childhood with his grandmother, and after the age of ten,
with his mother. His early years were bitter and cruel,
not only because of the poverty he knew, but because
of the repressive nature of the parochial education he
received. Jacques Borel began writing poetry at an early
age. After earning the usual degrees he started teaching
English at the lycées. In 1965, he wrote his first novel,
The Bond (L'Adoration) which won the much coveted
Goncourt prize. His second novel, *The Return (Le
Retour)*, was published in 1970.

Borel is an outspokenly anti-structuralist and anti-
"new wave" novelist. In fact, he is against any kind of
school or grouping. An arch individualist, he favors
"confession type" writing, which, he says, most people
disdain today, but which opens wide the hidden regions
within the soul.

Essayist, novelist, and poet, Jacques Borel is also
a dramatist. And this, despite the fact that he is "suspicious" of the theatre, wondering whether it does not
encourage a state of escapism.

Jacques Borel's first play, *Tata or Education*, opened
on February 15, 1972. Some critics likened his drama

to *King Ubu* because of its cutting edge and also its cruelty; others found it hilarious. All agreed on its profound ramifications for man and society.

Q.   Your childhood was painful. Can you tell us something about it?

A.   My life was painful, yet very simple and *ordinary*. I was an orphan, really; and this is, of course, an important consideration. My mother and I were very poor. I worked hard and early in life to help her out. There is a certain amount of banality in life itself: the years of boarding school were very difficult; the lycée; my studies at the Sorbonne; and the jobs which I held all along. I also taught English until 1967. My thesis was on G. M. Hopkins — first dissertation in France on this poet. Then marriage. Children.

   I always had a passion for poetry. This was perhaps instrumental in my becoming a critic of poetry. I write regularly for the *Nouvelle Revue Française* and for *Critique*. I try to approach poetry from an "inner realm." Yet, my critical faculties have been developed to such an extent that I have become very much aware of my own deficiencies, in terms of poetry. I gave up writing poetry for this reason. My first narrative writing was autobiographical. I began my first volume in a state of despair at the age of 36. It was published when I was 40. I was awarded the Goncourt prize for this work and I must confess, it was like a thunderbolt. I was horrified by the fact that my tragic life with my mother could have been turned into what I hate the most in this world — a best seller. A long silence followed. I tried to forget; to be forgotten.

Q.   Can you go into some detail about *The Bond* and *The Return?*

A.   *The Bond* and *The Return* are behind me now. They
contributed — as does all writing but not these two
works exclusively — in moulding or modifying my out-
look on life.   Since I am still in the process of
evolving, I really cannot talk to you about these
works themselves — I can, however, discuss my
growth in terms of my writing, my vision.

    The Return is really not a novel though people
have called it that. It is a type of lengthy and breath-
less meditation in which a personal history — with all
of the apparent narcissism inherent in this kind of
writing — has been, hopefully, overcome; and where
the destiny of a being confronts, obscurely, a distant,
ancestral forest of myths.   These novels were conceived as a type of autobiographical "summing up;"
The Bond and *The Return,* as part I and II and *The
Fascinated Ones* "would" be the third.   I say
"would" because I may perhaps yield to the very
profound and lancinating temptation of cutting up or
shattering the mold.   In fact, even before finishing
The Fascinated Ones, another large volume, *The
Journal of Ligenere* (Ligenere is the fictitious name
for a real and frightful place), to which I alluded
before, will have been published — January, 1973.

    I absolutely did not plan on writing *The Journal
of Ligenere;* certainly not with publication in mind.
I never even thought of such a possibility when I
started it.   I'm afraid I'm really not a "writer."
How could I be when the most savage, the most
pained and wounded parts of me — though I cannot
get along without writing as yet — challenge literature as a whole — and with all of its might; not in
the way the new disciplines are contesting literature, but in the sense that nearly all writing today,
even the finest, has become an ornament, a decor, a
game.   Whether the game is seductive and wins you
over to its side is of little import.   Perhaps writing
is an escape?   In my case, however, it is a question

of an authentic journal which I have kept regularly
for nearly twelve years – during the period when I
visited one of the most disinherited and neglected
places in the world: the psychiatric hospital where
my mother has been agonizing all this time. The
intervals between my visits, the memories of so
much suffering, of such injustice and misfortune
(hers, that of others, of all people) continues to
haunt me. After having experienced this kind of
pain, one's views of the world are completely upset.
Such an upheaval is certainly obvious in my writing –
whatever the current styles. Dostoyevsky was born
as a result of *The House of the Dead*.

What can I say? You will perhaps better understand my feelings if I quote King Lear, when he tears
off his clothes and cries out on the moors:

Is man no more than this.... Thou art the thing
itself: unaccommodated man is no more but such
a poor, bare, forked animal as thou art.

Off, off you lendings! Come, unbutton here!

I obey nothing else. Yes, everything in life
speeds by so quickly today. To lay *bare* (perhaps
this is already a death knell,) to strip off all alibis
(isn't literature or at least a certain type of literature an alibi?) all veils in writing. Yes, that's it,
I believe. To accomplish this cutting open from the
very beginning, no matter how embryonic the attempt
may be, and even if the end product fails.... This
is what I attempted in *The Bond* and even more so
in certain chapters in *The Return* – in terms of the
death of illusions, of myths. This type of approach
has been my constant command and has increased
in intensity and depth with time.

How can this kind of writing be labelled "narrative," particularly if one is absolutely bent on
honesty and veracity? How can one not challenge
writing itself? An author must try to go still further
even if it means going to the extreme, that is, of

sacrificing, of even killing writing itself?   That's what my *Journal* really is.

Now you see that it is much more than a "document" or a "testimony."   It is a meditation on an experience pushed to the extreme — not abstractely conceived nor willed, nor even deliberate, but rather linked to the very breath of another being, born from the most unsharable contact with the most cutting of agonies — on pain *and* writing.   My amazement and my indignation vis a vis myself *and* my writing stemmed from the fact that I was unable to understand how my writing (far from being smothered within the embryo or choked up within some kind of feelings of nothingness emerging from one's own inanity in terms of the primordial wound, the incomprehensible and mortal wound of living), had become, at least for a while, more vigorous and more motivated.

You understand now why writing which "uses" situations and experiences. seems meaningless to me — though the temptation. of seeing an autobiographical "summation" through to the end is great — and why this kind of expression fills me with a type of shame, revulsion, and horror.

I have frequently repeated two of Kafka's phrases which once again come to mind.   Both of them appear in *Meditations on Sin, Suffering, Hope and the True Way*.   The first: "There is no having, there is only a being, a being who longs for the last sigh, for suffocation."

To write books, to pile them up, to create a "work," to dream of taking one's place in the history of literature, is to orient oneself not toward being, which is what I had believed for so long (Rilke's "To sing is to be."), but rather toward having, to realize that writing (the anguish of writing, the anguish of living — and nothing can separate these two in my mind) can one day become the source of having and constitute having itself.

The other Kafka phrase: "Nothing is real except the light that shines on a grotesque face as it withdraws, nothing else." It seems to me that we are confronted with this unbearable "face" today and we must cope with it, we must come to grips with it. It is on this level that the voice within me indicates the very area where my "work" is to come into being—without it there would be nothing but ruin, an inability to finish, a hopelessness which comes from a feeling of having reached the very edge of a terrible abyss, before which one is not yet able to rebel (or else, it's the same ceaseless, unanswerable questioning) and from which one knows that no withdrawal is possible anymore.

Q.   Why and how did you begin writing for the theatre?

A.   When I was young, I dreamt—as do many others—of being an actor. It seemed that I had the "voice" for it. I even took some courses in acting, but it was obvious that I was not suited for this profession. You can succeed as an actor only if you know how to make people laugh; I only know how to make my children laugh!

I really don't believe I like the theatre. After the publication of *The Bond* the French radio asked me to write a play. I said no, because I was certain I had no talent for writing and, furthermore, I had no desire to write for the theatre. There is not one dialogue in my novels—and this despite my ability to record voices, thoughts, inflections, as though I I had a recording machine implanted within me noting everything down and with *terrible* precision. I really don't like dialogue in novels or other forms. Dialogue: to listen to others in life, to the most insignificant details and despite Nathalie Sarraute's *tropisms*. Yet, the unconscious wager... I wrote my play, *Tata*, in one fell swoop—in two weeks.

Q. Who is and what is Tata?

A. The aunt in my story. Let me quote something I wrote about *Tata*: "*Tata* is the sad story of a young man, Charles, killed by kindness. He is a "child of sin." He is just going on 18 years of age; but his mother, Josephe, and his aunt, Albine, treat him like a child, and keep him locked up in a home isolated from the world. They wash him, comb his hair, dress him. They are always there, day and night. They never leave him out of their sight. For Albine — Charles must be saved from the sin to which Josephe had succombed long ago. Charles, however, seems to be playing a game; his reading of the books by the Countess de Ségur, which he found hidden away some-place, encourages him to create a most unusual fantasy world. Equally unusual is the form his rebellion is to take.

I would like to quote a statement made by one of the critics concerning this play: "This farce of un-paralleled violence is highly dramatic.... The author has recourse to a gigantic caricature, to an imaginary creation, analogous to King Ubu's universe. He places the "cocoon-like" family unit on trial. The theme of this farce is simple: a woman has made a mistake eighteen years ago. The fruit of her sin, Charles, has been brought up in a cottony, anesthetic-like universe by his mother, and, praticularly by his aunt, Tata, one of these monstrous women from whom nudity — even Christ's nudity on the cross, is a mortal sin. Jacques Borel's merit comes from the fact that he has accepted the enormous ramifications of such notions with all of their logical consequences. A woolen sweater will clothe the crucifix above Charles' bed. Only the head of Christ will be visible."

Tata: You see how flighty even bishops and priests can be. When the young girls go to confession and see this . . .

> how can you expect people not to
> expose themselves on the beaches? ...
Alas, in spite of the fact that Charles wore diapers
until he was 7 years old, despite the fact that he was
isolated from his neighbors, from the world, from
life, that his only outside contact were the novels of
the Countess de Ségur he grew. Ignoble nature took
hold of him. With Borel's terribly subjective logic,
Tata draws an analogy between Charles and her cat
whose carnal lust she has succeeded in destroying
by "operating" on him herself, and bravely with a
scissors, and transforming him into "an angelic
companion." What will Charles' fate be?"

Q. Is *Tata* autobiographical?

A. Jean Vauthier in a radio interview wanted me to
admit that it was. He probably believed that it was.
He certainly is not the only one who thought so.
But I say it is not. I am neither castrated, as Charles
is, nor am I an exhibitionist as he turns out to be —
nor even an illegitimate child. But it is true, as it
is with many young French children within the last
century, I did read the novels of the Comtesse de
Ségur. According to modern psychiatrists, her volumes are filled with sadism. In Sartre's magazine,
Modern Times, there was a fine article on the so-
called "edifying," aristocratic and very Catholic
Countess — author for nice children. Certainly her
characters are, to a great extent, at the root of my
farces. I have tried to mock the "wise" and com-
placent. This does not imply that I am not *also*
trying to settle my personal accounts in this play,
as in my novel, *The Bond*, with my own religious and
so-called well-meaning education.

I must admit that there is an apparent ferocity
in *Tata* and my other works: pity, what Dostoyevsky
called, in *The Idiot*, compassion.

Q.   Do you go to rehearsals or to the theatre in general?

A.   No, because the theatre fills me with an oppressive
feeling of futility, almost in the Pascalian sense of
"diversion." I prefer to read the few plays that are
meaningful to me by myself. To have a silent tête-
a-tête with them, as one does with all books. I was
asked to attend the rehearsals of *Tata*. In fact, I
was almost forced to go. I did make a few suggestions.

I "saw" Tata, I heard her, I seemed to know her.
I was vaguely disturbed, because no actress could
really incarnate her properly — there are always differences.   Nevertheless, Tata played by Denise
Gence, one of the finest actresses of the Comédie-
Française, was truly remarkable. My only suggestion
was to insist upon the chatty side of the character,
voluble, the "Marquise" side of Tata. She is one
of those beings who drowns everything out — all
truth — she levels everything under the flow of her
innocuous verbiage. I think that this kind of person
is well known to the psychoanalyst.

I also begged the director not to play Tata in a
realistic way. Perhaps certain scenes or episodes
may appear realistic no matter how mad they are,
but to play them this way would lead to error. Madness or the *dream* is the culminating point of my
play. Of Charles' poetic reveries, with his imaginary
friends. And *not* realism.

Q.   What about the actors?

A.   I had a good time with them. It was a milieu I did
not know. We had lunch and dinner almost every day
together. Even in life, actors are astonishing. We
really never know when they stop playing — perhaps
they are not even aware of it. That's why they are
so fascinating.

Q.   What dramatists have influenced you most incisively?

A.   The only ones I really love are the Greek tragic
dramatists.   That's really theatre: the confrontation
of man and destiny.   Shakespeare also.   But even in
Shakespeare there is a deteriorating relationship
between man and destiny, and the sacred.   And that's
why he is so modern.   Jan Knott was right to insist
upon this point in *Shakespeare, Our Contemporary*.
Finally, Racine: he's the only one probably, at least
in *Phaedra*, who is able to place man — in terms of
the sacred — face to face with his destiny.
     My play, therefore, may seem to be only an
"incomprehensible" caricature.   Or perhaps, the
times warrant such notions — because everything that
is sacred has gotten the hell out of the theatre.   If
I have written a modern play without realizing it,
it's because I am part of my century, subject to the
same anguishes, sensitive to derision.   And now to
explain myself: I can take the mockery Freud made
of Sophocles' great Oedipus myth.

Q.   What about novelists?

A.   Outside of Dostoyevsky and Tolstoi, I really don't
like fiction.   I only like autobiographies, which are
frowned upon today, particularly in France.   It's
like introducing a little truth into the lie.   The
Rousseau of the *Confessions* or of the *Reveries*,
or Proust... These are examples of autobiographies.

Q.   Why did you call *Tata* a moralistic and didactic play?

A.   Because it is a jarring farce.   We can find a common
denominator between Molière in this respect and
Tata — both are satires of a certain kind of education,
so destructive in so many cases: bourgeois, Catholic,
puritan.   This kind of education is on the way out,

although it still exists in certain Latin countries; but the reaction today (a logical outcome) is at the opposite poles — and is equally oppressive.

Q. You have specific ideas concerning comedy. Can you elaborate on these?

A. Each time I think of the theatre, it's in terms of comedy — clownish things.   Cruel farces, in a half dreamlike style.   A play in which madness is the pivotal point, which makes one laugh until it tears your heart out — until it becomes unbearable.
     No, not Ionesco-type comedy. It would be more Molière-type humor. I remember when I was a child, I cried when I saw *School for Wives*. I have wanted to write something about this play for years.

Q. Since you are a novelist, would you consider yourself part of the "new wave" group alluded to by some as the *école du regard*.

A. I hate the word and the notion. "New wave" sounds to me like a TV ad for a toothpaste or some gadget — newer and brighter. I despise so-called schools or groups.   These groups are a French phenomena perhaps — the product of pedants.   Why école du regard?   Why a school at all?   Kafka was alone. Bernanos, Céline was alone. Baudelaire. Nerval. Faulkner. My answer to this question is contained in my second novel, *The Return*, where I describe the house in which I once lived, piece by piece, object by object. In an implacably precise manner. And yet, it's the opposite of the *école du regard*. Objects do not interest me. Nor do they move me. People do. I'm perhaps very much isolated these days. This may be unfortunate or it may be for the best. I hate technique for technique's sake. Pascal and Claudel said the last word on this subject.

So did Rousseau. I abhor those who smirk at Solzhenitsyn. Is it he or they who are the bourgeois?
Because *his* art is not like toothpaste — ''newer and
brighter.''

Q.   Are your characters logical? Irrational? Symbolistic?
     or shadows? How could you describe them?

A.   All characters seem to me to be both logical and
     irrational. We can look at the terrible logic of the
     insane — namely the paranoics. It's when the ir-
     rational distrubs everything, creates a state of chaos,
     that I'm fascinated. All characters are symbolic and
     real, physical and shadow-like. If a character were
     conceived only as a symbol, it would not hold to-
     gether. If Don Quixote were merely a symbol, he
     would have vanished a long time ago. The same can
     be said for Hamlet, the Brothers Karamazov, and
     Faulkner's characters.
         I would like to believe in the reality of my char-
     acters. Little by little I come to realize or experience
     the deep crevices within their personalities, the
     disquieting, dangerous, inner world.

Q.   What about modern directors, like Lavelli? Drama-
     tists like Arrabal?

A.   I live like a hermit, in the country, with my wife and
     five children. I rarely go to the theatre or to the
     movies. I must admit, however, that I'm very much
     impressed with Lavelli's *mises-en-scène* and also
     with Arrabal's theatre. Arrabal's novel, *Baal Baby-
     lone*, touched me very deeply. I told you about my
     passion for autobiography, even if it's half imaginary.
     Because of the dangerous depths to which it leads
     the reader and the sudden aperture into the most
     vertiginous depths. I have a passion for confessional

literature.   Adamov is greater as an autobiographer
than he is as a dramatist.   *Man and Child* is truly
remarkable.   As far as his plays are concerned, they
can be interpreted any way — the way the wind blows.

Q.   What are your future plans?

A.   I've been asked to write some plays and probably
will.   And yet, I'm still "suspicious" of the theatre.
I keep thinking of it as a type of escape mechanism.